ENGLISH LITERATURE
GCSE Grade Booster

Stephen Papworth

Schofield & Sims Ltd.

© 1990 Schofield & Sims Ltd.

All rights reserved.
No part of this publication may be
reproduced, stored in a retrieval system, or
transmitted, in any form, or by any means,
electronic, mechanical, photocopying,
recording or otherwise, without the prior
permission of Schofield & Sims Ltd.

0 7217 4616 0

First printed 1990

Schofield & Sims Ltd.
Dogley Mill
Fenay Bridge
Huddersfield
HD8 0NQ
England

Typeset by Ocean, Leeds
Printed in Great Britain by the Alden Press, Oxford

Contents

Introduction: Studying English Literature   5
English Language and English Literature – Why Study Literature? – What You Learn in an English Literature Course – How English Literature Is Assessed – Reading About Texts

1 **Reading Prose**   10
Passage Questions – Unseen Appreciation – How to Tackle Unseen Prose – Answering the Questions

2 **Understanding Plays, Novels and Short Stories**   26
Getting the Full Picture – Character – Relationships – Settings – Themes – Plot – Making Notes – Plays, Films and Videos

3 **Writing About Plays, Novels and Short Stories**   42
Forms of Assessment – Worked Exercises

4 **Getting the Most from Poetry**   64
What Poetry Is – The Techniques of Poetry – A Warning – Tackling a Poem

5 **Writing About Poetry**   79
How to Write About a Poem – Worked Exercise

6 **Wider Reading**   85
Personal Responses – Choosing Texts and Topics – Getting the Best out of Your Teacher – Wider Reading Essay – Creative Work in Wider Reading – The Value of Wider Reading

Index   96

Acknowledgements

The author and the publishers wish to thank the following for permission to use copyright material:

Laurie Lee for an extract from *Cider with Rosie*, published by Chatto & Windus.

The Estate of F. Scott Fitzgerald for an extract from *The Great Gatsby*, published by The Bodley Head.

Elaine Green Ltd. for an extract from *Death of a Salesman* by Arthur Miller, published by Penguin Books. Copyright ©1949 by Arthur Miller.

Bill Naughton for an extract from *Spring and Port Wine*.

Samuel French Ltd. for extracts from *Hobson's Choice* by Harold Brighouse, published by Heinemann Educational. No performances of the whole or an extract of the play may be performed without prior permission from Samuel French Ltd.

The Marvell Press, England, for the quotations from the poem *Toads* by Philip Larkin, from "The Less Deceived".

Carcanet Press Ltd. for an extract from the poem *Cracking Icicles in Totley Tunnel* by Ian McMillan, from "Selected Poems".

Faber & Faber Ltd. for an extract from the poem *On the Move* by Thom Gunn, from "The Sense of Movement", and an extract from the poem *Look, Stranger*, from "The Collected Poems of W. H. Auden".

James MacGibbon for *Not Waving But Drowning*, from "The Collected Poems of Stevie Smith" (Penguin 20th Century Classics).

Introduction: Studying English Literature

English Language and English Literature

At GCSE level, English is divided into two subjects – *English* (often called *English Language*) and *English Literature*. Usually, students have to take two different assessments for these two qualifications, though some examining groups are introducing dual certification courses, in which one extended assessment programme will give students the chance of both qualifications. Whichever it is, if you are doing English Literature, you will need to think a little about the nature of the subject.

What, then, is English Literature, and how is it different from English Language?

Literature can be thought of as imaginative writing – such things as novels, short stories, plays and poems. Not every example would qualify as literature, however, since the term is used only for writing that is considered good of its kind. Thus, in English Literature courses you will study books judged by experts to have been written by especially imaginative or perceptive authors. It is clear that you study texts like this in all English courses, but in English Language courses the texts are studied alongside many other forms of writing such as newspaper articles, letters, and factual essays. In English Literature courses, you will only have imaginative writing to deal with, and you will mostly be expected to read whole books. What is more, rather than doing your own creative writing, you will be working mainly on exercises and essays about the meaning of these books, how they are written, and how they affect you. You may, however, also get the chance to write imaginatively, but it will always be in a way closely related to the books that you have read.

Why Study Literature?

In English Literature classes, your teachers are trying to interest you in literature, to give you the skills you need to read it with pleasure, and to make sure you understand what you are studying. They believe literature is worthwhile in several ways.

1. Reading literature puts you in touch with the minds of very imaginative writers: this can give pleasure, but also it may expand your imagination, changing the way in which you think.

2. There may be wisdom to be gained from literature by looking at the way in which good writers think about life.

3. Since authors of literature often have something complex to say, they use language in unusual and effective ways. By studying the ways in which they write, you can improve your skills at both reading and writing.

What You Learn in an English Literature Course

The subject of the GCSE course is *how to read* literature. The course is only secondarily concerned with what authors say, and only incidentally with what other people say about the authors. Thus, the main activities involved will be reading, and writing about, the texts you are set. In certain syllabuses, you will have to learn some facts about the texts for examinations; but even then you will gain most marks by showing how *you* understand the texts, and how you personally react to them. Your response to the texts is all-important.

Not just any response will do, however. There are skills in reading that help you spot which responses the author wanted you to have, and one of the main aims of this book is to help you with these skills. One of the major causes of eccentric responses to books or poems, however, is very simple: a text may describe an experience that is in some way very similar to one of your own; or it may use a word or phrase that has some private meaning to you because of the way someone you know uses it. When you read this, your first reaction may be to suppose it has the same meaning to the author, and to people in general, when it probably does not: you will have given the text *your* meaning, not the one that would be

What You Learn in an English Literature Course

given to it by most good readers. It really pays to be aware of this "private meanings trap" when you are thinking about your reactions.

In all syllabuses, you will study prose, drama and poetry. This book covers all three topics. (Prose is any form of connected writing that is not poetry: in English Literature it usually means novels, short stories and biographies.) There are several ways of studying each topic.

First of all, you need to grasp the detail of how writers work, how they control meanings and influence your feelings. You can study this by working on passages from set books, or by reading passages of authors whose work you have never seen before. In written exercises, your responses can be in the form of essays; or, more usually, answers to questions. Every syllabus uses both of these types of passage, and the skills you will learn by tackling them are basic to the other forms of study which follow.

A second type of study consists of writing about a single text or an aspect of a single text. The types of essay that are set on these lines vary from book reviews in which you sum up your reactions to a text, through studies of aspects of the content of the text (character, settings, ideas, feelings and so on), to studies of the author's style and techniques throughout the text. Mostly your essays will be explanations of how you understand the text or how you react to it, but you may be given the opportunity to write as if you were a character or an author. Sometimes, you may be given a series of short-answer questions instead. This type of work on single texts is generally known as *Intensive Study*.

YOUR RESPONSE IS WHAT MATTERS.

Finally, all GCSE Literature syllabuses test you on reading of your own choice, in exercises known as *Open Studies* or *Wider Reading*. For these you will be expected to read books on your own (often from lists of titles

suggested by your teacher) and write about them, either one at a time, or, more usually, in groups of two or three texts, where you are asked about what they have in common, or how they differ. The regulations for this type of work vary widely between syllabuses: make sure you know exactly what *you* need to do as you read the chapter on Wider Reading.
- *Your* understanding and *your* responses will gain you most marks: learning facts is secondary.

How English Literature Is Assessed

With many of the types of exercise mentioned, a single title or set of questions can test students right across the range of abilities. Occasionally, however, separate exercises may be set for the more able and less able to do. All of the types of exercise can be set as coursework, or as part of an examination.

Most syllabuses have two sections, one assessed by a *coursework* folder, and one assessed by an *examination*. The sort of work you will do will be similar for both sections, but work on set books for examinations will lead to some learning of facts for the exam. How much and just what you have to learn depends on the type of examination. *Open-book examinations* allow you to take your text into the examination room: in this case you will need to have basic facts about the text in your head, and know where to find the passages that illustrate them. For other examinations, you will need to learn by heart some quotations from the text to illustrate the things you know. Just how much you need to learn depends on the way the questions are set, so ask your teacher to let you see some old examination papers before you plan your revision. In all normal syllabuses, your Wider Reading studies form part of the coursework.

A few syllabuses exist without any coursework at all, but these are only for external students – people who have left school and who are not attending a college.

Finally, there are a few coursework-only syllabuses, which give teachers the best opportunity of setting work for individual students' benefit. These syllabuses tend to take up a great deal of students' time, however, so do not feel disappointed if you are not doing one.

Find out the requirements of your syllabus in detail:
- How many coursework assignments do you have to do?
- What is assessed by coursework and what by examination?
- What are the regulations for Wider Reading?
- What types of questions are set in examinations?
- Can you take texts into examination rooms?

Reading About Texts

Bookshop shelves – probably not far from the ones where you found this book – usually contain many brightly-coloured booklets on GCSE English Literature texts. Using these booklets is not cheating, but they need to be treated with caution if they are to be helpful to you. The problem is that they are mainly about *what a text contains*, rather than about *how to come to understand it for yourself.* They tend to be crammed full of information about plots, characters and style, without really helping you to understand these things for yourself.

This *Grade Booster*, on the other hand, is a "*how to*" book: it refers to texts only in order to help you to see things for yourself. It refers to books that you may not have read, but in such a way as to teach you how to think independently about any book.

If you have some reading skills, conventional "crib" books can be a great help in deciding what you yourself think, and in choosing what to revise. They are no substitute for reading, and thinking about, a text for yourself, however: second-hand views will stand out a mile in your essay, and will attract hardly any marks at all. By all means read these books, but use them intelligently.

- In assignments, never simply copy work out of "crib" books, even if you put it into your own words. Such second-hand writing is easy for assessors to spot.

1 Reading Prose

Passage Questions

THE EARLIEST FORM OF LITERATURE.

On the whole, students find novels, short stories and biographies the easiest forms of literature to study, and it is not difficult to see why. Whilst plays need to be performed to come fully alive, and poetry often uses language in complex ways, prose is intended to be read fairly quickly. Moreover, novels, short stories and biographies are close to the most basic form of story-telling that we all enjoy – gossip, which is as old as the human race. Nevertheless, good stories are written with thought and care, and often with genius, so they really need reading with great attention if the full sense and feeling is to be got out of them.

You will need to read your set books with more than everyday thoughtfulness if you are to write good essays on them, but in any case the habit of thoughtful reading will actually enable you to get more enjoyment out of books in general. To encourage these skills, all GCSE English Literature syllabuses contain opportunities to study and answer questions on passages of prose taken from books that you are not studying for other parts of the syllabus. These so-called *unseen appreciation* questions may be found in either the coursework or the examined sections of a syllabus.

Additional exercises may be set on passages from your set books. Because it is possible to set several short questions on a passage, some much easier than others, this type of passage-question allows teachers to test both the weakest and brightest students in their classes. In the examination room, you may find you are presented with exercises where a passage is printed and several short questions are set, as an alternative to full-length essays. If your syllabus has an open-book examination, you will be told which part of your text to read, and only the questions will be printed on the examination paper.

- You can use the skills learnt in unseen questions to help make notes on your set books.
- By the end of the course you should be reading more thoughtfully and applying these skills almost without thinking about it.

Unseen Appreciation

An unseen exercise looks like this – though in an examination there would probably be fewer questions. Read it through twice, and think about the questions.

Read the following passage carefully and answer the questions that follow.

I had sat well back on the form, and while seeming to be busy with my sum, had held my slate in such a manner as to conceal my face: I might have escaped notice, had not my treacherous slate somehow happened to slip from my hand, and falling with an obtrusive crash, directly drawn every eye upon me; I knew it was all over now, and, as I stooped to pick up the two fragments of slate, I rallied my forces for the worst. It came.

"A careless girl!" said Mr. Brocklehurst, and immediately after – "It is the new pupil, I perceive." And before I could draw breath, "I must not forget I have a word to say respecting her." Then aloud: how loud it seemed to me! "Let the child who broke her slate, come forward!"

Of my own accord, I could not have stirred; I was paralysed: but the two great girls who sat on each side of me, set me on my legs and pushed me towards the dread judge, and then Miss Temple gently assisted me to his very feet, and I caught her whispered counsel –

"Don't be afraid, Jane, I saw it was an accident; you shall not be punished."

The kind whisper went to my heart like a dagger.

"Another minute, and she will despise me for a hypocrite," thought I; and an impulse of fury against Reed, Brocklehurst, and Co. bounded in my pulses at the conviction. I was no Helen Burns.

"Fetch that stool," said Mr. Brocklehurst, pointing to a very high one from which a monitor had just risen: it was brought.

"Place the child upon it."

And I was placed there, by whom I don't know: I was in no condition to note particulars; I was only aware that they had hoisted me to the height of Mr. Brocklehurst's nose, that he was within a yard of me, and that a spread of shot orange and purple silk pelisses[1], and a cloud of silvery plumage extended and waved below me.

Mr. Brocklehurst hemmed.

"Ladies," said he, turning to his family; "Miss Temple, teachers, and children, you see this girl?"

Of course they did; for I felt their eyes directed like burning-glasses against my scorched skin.

"You see she is yet young; you observe she possesses the ordinary form of childhood; God has graciously given her the shape that He has given to all of us; no signal deformity points her out as a marked character. Who would think that the Evil One had already found a servant and agent in her? Yet such, I grieve to say, is the case."

A pause – in which I began to steady the palsy[2] of my nerves, and to feel that the Rubicon[3] was passed; and that the trial, no longer to be shirked, must be firmly sustained.

"My dear children," pursued the black marble clergyman, with pathos, "this is a sad, a melancholy[4] occasion; for it becomes my duty to warn you, that this girl, who might be one of God's own lambs, is a little castaway: not a member of the true flock, but evidently an interloper and an alien. You must be on your guard against her; you must shun her example; if necessary, avoid her company, exclude her from your sports, and shut her out from your converse. Teachers, you must watch her: keep your eyes on her movements, weigh well her words, scrutinise her actions, punish her body to save her soul: if, indeed, such salvation be possible, for (my tongue falters while I tell it) this girl, this child, the native of a Christian land, worse than many a little heathen who says its prayers to Brahma[5] and kneels before Juggernaut[6] – this girl is – a liar!"

1. *pelisses*: long, loose cloaks, often sleeveless
2. *palsy*: fit of trembling
3. *Rubicon*: point of no return
4. *melancholy*: gloomy
5. *Brahma*: a Hindu god
6. *Juggernaut*: a Hindu idol

1. Trace the changes in Jane's feelings as the scene progresses. Refer to individual words and phrases that you think convey these feelings.
2. Describe Mr. Brocklehurst's tone as he talks to Jane (a) when she breaks her slate, and (b) when she is out in front of the class.
3. Jane is very young when this scene occurs. What can you tell about her character from the passage? Show which words and phrases convey her character to you.
4. This is a small incident, but may still seem quite dramatic to you. Write down what you think might give it this dramatic quality.

Let us consider what the questions are looking for.

How to Tackle Unseen Prose

One of the first things we notice about this unseen is the help that is given in the notes about difficult vocabulary. Not all Examining Groups will give this help, but it does point to a difference between unseen appreciation exercises and comprehensions. The questions here are not generally about the basic meaning of words and phrases; they are about the feelings the words create in your mind as you read them, the hints you take from them, or the sense that the passage as a whole adds up to. In the next few pages, we will study how words work in these ways.

Words, Beliefs and Feelings

When you look up a word in a dictionary, you expect to find its meaning – that is, a statement of what aspect of reality it refers to. Thus, "loose coat or cloak" is the meaning of *pelisse*, "gloomy" the meaning of *melancholy*, and so on. But words carry many more layers of meaning than can be stated in a simple definition. You can see this if you compare an everyday word with a list of other words having the same basic meanings. Such words are called *synonyms*.

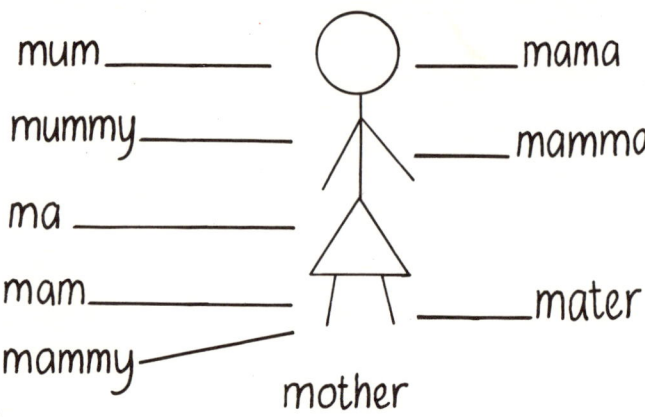

All the words in the diagram mean the same thing at a basic level: a woman who has a child. This basic level of meaning is called the *denotation* of each word. It is clear, though, that on another level the following two sentences do not mean quite the same thing:

Is that your mother?
Is that your mummy?

Perhaps at this point you should pause for a moment and try to work out just what the difference is.

"Is that your mother?" can be taken as a purely factual enquiry, whereas "Is that your mummy?" is tinged with feeling – the comforting, reassuring attitude that people sometimes adopt when talking to a child. It has this effect because we know that *mummy* is a word which we normally use with children. "Is that your mam?" and "Is that your mamma?" would have different effects still. We know about both of these words, that they are normally used with children but that *mam* is more often used by working-class people in the North of England, and that *mamma* is an old-fashioned word which was used by upper-class people. Thus, although both the words carry suggestions of tenderness or childishness like *mummy*, each hints to us different ideas about the writer or speaker, and the circumstances in which he or she is speaking. The feelings, attitudes and beliefs suggested by a word are its *connotations*.

- Words and phrases carry two orders of meaning: (a) their basic level of meaning (denotation), and (b) the feelings, attitudes and beliefs at which they hint (connotations).
- Synonyms are words with the same denotation, but they almost always each have different connotations.

You may like to pause now and think about what might be suggested by using the words *ma, mum, mama, mammy* and *mater*.

Most words have more than one denotation, and more than one set of connotations: when you read, you choose the meanings that best fit into the rest of the passage you are looking at. If you are faced by a word that you think might be important because of its connotations, try substituting a synonym in its place in the passage:

> The judge said to the murderer, "Yours was an exceptionally wicked deed."

If you wished to investigate *wicked*, you could substitute a synonym:

> The judge said to the murderer, "Yours was an exceptionally naughty deed."

This might make you smile because the childish connotations are so inappropriate: it reveals how serious a word *wicked* is in the context.

- When puzzled about the connotations of a word or phrase, use the *substitution test*.

Comparisons

Words often release their connotations most powerfully when they are used in comparisons, of which there are several basic types in literature. Together with symbols they are known as *imagery*.

Similes are comparisons linked together by the words *as* or *like*. In his story "The Prussian Officer", D. H. Lawrence wrote:

> Gradually the officer had become aware of his servant's young, vigorous, unconscious presence about him . . . It was like a warm flame upon the older man's tense, rigid body, that had become almost unliving, fixed.

Here, the simile of heat makes us think of liveliness and human warmth, and of the irritation this quality might produce in the old, cold officer.

Metaphors are comparisons where the *like* or *as* has been missed out. They are harder to spot than similes, but are even more common. In another story, "The Fox", D. H. Lawrence writes about a woman whose fiancé has just killed her friend:

> She stood there absolutely helpless, shuddering her dry sobs and her mouth trembling rapidly. And then, as in a child, with a little crash came the tears and the blind agony of sightless weeping.

Tears cannot literally *crash*, either in the sense of making a loud noise or in the sense of smashing into something; therefore, *crash* must be a metaphor comparing the coming of the tears to a crash. The connotations of violence and of shock are applied to the tears: the feelings the woman got from them were *like* those she might get from a crash, so the metaphor is appropriate and adds to the distressing feelings portrayed by the passage.

Personifications are metaphors or similes in which something non-human is described as if it were something human. When Dylan Thomas describes the part of Swansea where he grew up as "a snug, smug, trim, middling-prosperous suburb", we may note that *smug* is a word that can really only be applied to human beings. It vividly and immediately describes the sort of life which is lived there. In general, personifications portray either the human connotations of what is described, or the author's reactions to it.

Symbols

Similes, metaphors and personifications are not the only ways in which one thing can be made to stand for another. In all of these figures of speech, something imaginary is substituted for something real: in the two examples from D. H. Lawrence (page 15), the servant's "presence" was real and the flame imaginary, just as the violence of the woman's tears was real and the crash was imaginary. When something real in a story reminds us of something else, we call it a symbol.

Traditional Symbols. In everyday speech we have many stock phrases where one thing stands for another. The link between the two ideas can be metaphorical, or there may be some other form of association between the two. For instance, scales are a symbol for justice because they resemble justice in being balanced and fair; lions, on the other hand, symbolise strength and courage not because they are like these qualities, but because they possess them. Doves symbolise peace because they are not predators and make a soothing sound. You should be able to spot traditional symbols whenever they occur, and explain the connection between them and their meanings. Their effect is generally to make writing more concrete, to give the mind something solid to grasp on, instead of an abstract idea.

Fire is the traditional symbol for life, passion and defiance; and darkness a symbol for death. In *The Return of the Native*, Thomas Hardy uses them with these meanings, when the villagers of Egdon Heath light their autumn bonfires.

> The first tall flame from Rainbarrow sprang into the sky, attracting all eyes that had been fixed on the distant conflagrations back to their own attempt in the same kind. The cheerful blaze streaked the inner surface of the human circle – now increased by other stragglers, male and female – with its own gold livery, and even overlaid the dark turf around with a lively luminousness, which softened off into obscurity where the barrow rounded downwards out of sight . . .
> . . . To light a fire is the instinctive and resistant act of man when, at the winter ingress, the curfew is sounded throughout Nature.

Hardy chooses to hint at the symbols' meanings here, but their force is felt because they are well known to us. Note that the fires are really present in the imaginary world of the story.

New Symbols. Sometimes you may become aware that an author is writing about something at a greater length than at first seems justified, or perhaps keeps returning to an idea in the course of a work. In cases like these, ask yourself whether the author intends it to stand for something else. Consider what it resembles, what its connotations are, and what else in the text it shares characteristics with. In *Bleak House*, Charles Dickens writes at great length about a London fog, and the reader may wonder why the author is so fascinated by it. It is only when Dickens describes it hovering round the lawyers' offices and courts at Temple Bar and Lincoln's Inn that its connotations come alive and we can guess at its meaning:

> The raw afternoon is rawest, and the dense fog is densest . . . near that leaden-headed old obstruction . . . Temple Bar. And hard by Temple Bar, in Lincoln's Inn Hall, at the very heart of the fog, sits the Lord High Chancellor in his High Court of Chancery.

Fog, like the lawyers, is an obstruction: it gets in the way, obscures things and slows them down, just as the book's lawyers do. Fog, therefore, is a symbol for the law.

- Comparisons and symbols affect our reactions by transferring our feelings from one thing to another. When dealing with comparisons and symbols, try to explain what the feelings are, and why they are important. (Never simply list the imagery you have found: always describe its effects.)

Tone, Mood and Characterisation

Authors often have long-term aims when they manipulate the meanings in a passage:
- they may be trying to adopt an overall tone of voice (friendly, humorous or tragic, for instance);
- they may be trying to create a mood (such as happiness or misery);
- they may be trying to characterise a speaker (as friendly, excitable or middle-class, for instance).

If you can spot these long-term intentions, you will be awarded more marks.

In Wilkie Collins's *The Woman in White*, Walter Hartright describes the young woman he has fallen in love with. It is shortly before their enforced separation.

> She was dressed in a brown cloak, with a plain black silk gown under it. On her head was the same simple straw hat which she had worn on the morning when we first met. A veil was attached to it now which hid her face from me. By her side trotted a little Italian greyhound, the pet companion of all her walks, smartly dressed in a scarlet cloth wrapper, to keep the sharp air from his delicate skin. She did not seem to notice the dog. She walked straight forward, with her head drooping a little, and her arms folded in her cloak. The dead leaves, which had whirled in the wind before me when I had heard of her marriage engagement in the morning, whirled in the wind before her, and rose and fell and scattered themselves at her feet as she walked on in the pale waning sunlight. The dog shivered and trembled, and pressed against her dress impatiently for notice and encouragement. But she never heeded him. She walked on, farther and farther away from me, with the dead leaves whirling about her on the path – walked on, till my aching eyes could see her no more, and I was left alone again with my own heavy heart.

The mood of depression in this passage is created by the consistent use of words with depressing connotations. It starts with the two dull, muted colours, brown and black, which suggest the young woman's dull mood: she is almost in mourning, almost in hiding from the world, as is suggested by her wearing a veil. The wintry, bleak morning is skilfully evoked to intensify this mood: the reader's attention is repeatedly drawn to the leaves, which are "dead", and to the wind which "whirls" them round in an almost ghost-like manner. The sun is out, but its light is "waning" or declining, contributing to the feeling of misery. We are told that "the dog shivered and trembled", and though this is because of the cold, we still feel that it is sharing in the misery. Finally, Hartright's physical sensations are described – his "aching eyes" and "heavy heart" – which really bring his sadness home.

There is one note of contrast with all this sadness, the greyhound's smart "scarlet cloth wrapper", which might be expected to bring a note of brightness and gaiety to the description; here, however, it simply adds to the feeling of depression because it is such a contrast with the passage's general feeling.

Wilkie Collins's purpose in writing this passage goes further, however: he is deepening our picture of Hartright's character through it. Several incidents that come earlier in the novel show him to be a passionate, romantic young man, and here the feeling of despair showing through his description of the girl confirms this characterisation to us. Even when reading an unseen passage, you should be looking for this type of character-drawing.

Descriptive Power

Often a description will depend for its effectiveness on the moods and feelings it contains, but there is another way in which descriptions can be made vivid. Words normally represent things in the outside world, but we can choose words that represent the basic information given to us by our senses. Such words refer to brightness, darkness, colour and shape, sounds, smells, tastes and touch-sensations. We call the use of words like this *sensuous language*. See how many sensuous words you can find in this passage from Laurie Lee's *Cider with Rosie*, describing a country garden at high summer.

> A tropic heat oozed up from the ground, rank with sharp odours of roots and nettles. Snow-clouds of elder-blossom banked in the sky, showering upon me the fumes and flakes of their sweet and giddy suffocation. High overhead ran frenzied larks, screaming, as though the sky were tearing apart.

"Heat" is an obvious word; but it is made much more vivid by "oozed" which makes us feel the slow warming of the body as it lies on warm earth. It also reminds us of perspiration. The odours of this garden are not sweet but "sharp", the true smells of weeds; but the smells of blossom are "fumes" of "giddy suffocation". This makes us imagine them as being so strong as to make us faint. Sight is involved in the images of "snow-clouds" and "flakes", and the violent sound of the birds is put over vividly by the unusual word "screaming". We can say that the passage as a whole is made vivid because of its sensuous language.

- Always check descriptions for sensuous words and phrases. Look for references to sight, sound, smell, taste, texture and temperature.
- Ask yourself if the sensuousness affects the passage's mood.

Other Means of Expression

Qualities of language other than those of meaning can affect a passage's impact. They are mentioned only briefly here as they are developed at greater length in the chapters on poetry.

The *sound of words* may be harsh or soft: *battle* sounds harsh, and is appropriate to war; *scratch* appropriately has a harsh sound; *sleep* and *song* are both soft. Occasionally words make the sound of the thing they represent: this is *onomatopoeia*. Some examples are *bang*, *jangle*, *swish* and *cuckoo*. In these ways the sounds of words can make passages more vivid.

The *length of sentences* can affect the mood of a passage. Short sentences can sound brusque, angry or choked with emotion, whilst long ones can convey subtleties of meaning or be pompous and long-winded. The precise feeling that we get from any one type of sentence depends, of course, on the connotations of the words it contains.

- The sounds of language can be almost as important in prose as in poetry.

Labelling: A Warning

This chapter has used some special words for the features found in good writing, such as metaphor, simile and sensuousness. Remember, though, that you will get little credit for simply listing the features you find in a passage: what your teacher or examiner wants to see is how they affect your response to it. You *must* try to write about how they affect your understanding of, and so your feelings about, what you have read.

- The importance of technical features lies only in the way they affect your response.

Answering the Questions

Now let's go back to the exercise printed on pages 11-13, and examine how to answer specific questions.

Q1. *Trace the changes in Jane's feelings as the scene progresses. Refer to individual words and phrases that you think convey these feelings.*

On one level, this question asks you to retell some of the content of the passage – the ways in which one feeling follows another during Jane's ordeal – and some of your references to words and phrases can simply show that feelings are mentioned. On another level, words and phrases may be found conveying feelings just because of their connotations, and much credit will be given for demonstrating this.

Feelings are in fact mentioned twice, in "I was paralysed", and "an impulse of fury . . . bounded in my pulses". As we read, however, we instantly know what Jane's feelings are at many other points because we respond to the connotations of what is written. The question might be answered as follows.

Answering the Questions

> *Answer*
> At first, Jane is shy and nervous: this is suggested to us by her sitting back and hiding her face, and by the way she drops her slate. Her feelings of dread come out when she knows "it was all over now," which suggests that she thinks a disaster is on hand. Fear is also suggested by her feeling "paralysed" with weakness and terror. More complex is the emotion when, as she says, Miss Temple's "kind whisper went to my heart like a dagger". The simile suggests instant pain, which occurs because she fears that the teacher will believe the accusations and think her "a hypocrite". This is followed by "fury" at her accusers, which we can imagine sensuously as it "bounded" in her pulses. At the same time she is stunned: this is suggested by her not knowing who lifted her up on to the stool. Embarrassment follows: this is again portrayed through sensuous references to her feeling hot as if her accusers' eyes were "burning-glasses" which "scorched" her. Finally comes courage, when she realises that the ordeal cannot be "shirked" but must be "sustained" or put up with: the word "shirk" suggests that wishing to escape from it would be like trying to escape from work.

This answer catalogues a series of feelings, as demanded by the question, which gains some marks; it links each feeling to a word or phrase, usually quoting it, for more marks; and it explains how that word or phrase works in terms of connotations (what is suggested) for yet more marks. Similes and sensuous language are noted, but only to help explain how words come to have their particular effects.

Q2. Describe Mr. Brocklehurst's tone as he talks to Jane (a) when she breaks her slate, and (b) when she is out in front of the class.

This question asks purely for your response to Mr. Brocklehurst's words: the answers lie less in what he says than in the tone of voice suggested by his words.

> *Answer*
> (a) When Jane drops her slate, Mr. Brocklehurst's tone must already be full of blame. His first words, "A careless girl!" are curt, and jump to the conclusion that she is at fault. His command, "Let the child who broke her slate, come forward!" is cold in tone: to call her "child" is colder than calling her "girl" or calling her by her name.

> (b) His tone when Jane is in front of the class is similar. He finds unkind words to call her ("castaway", "interloper" and "alien"); and his warnings make it sound as if she is dangerous:
>   "You must be on your guard against her; you must shun her example."
> "Shun" is a particularly cold and unkind word to use. In addition it is as if he is trying to sound holy, speaking of God and the Evil One. The beginning of his speech is very formal, almost like "My Lords, Ladies and Gentlemen", showing he is blowing the event up out of all proportion.

Notice here the use of terms to describe the emotional colour, or tone, of Mr. Brocklehurst's words: *full of blame*, *curt*, *cold*, *unkind*, *holy*, *formal*. In each case, an example is quoted to justify the use of these words, and a few words of explanation are given. Also notice how the comparison of the effects of "girl" and "child" are an example of the use of the substitution test.

Q3. *Jane is very young when this scene occurs. What can you tell about her character from the passage? Show which words and phrases convey her character to you.*

Character questions like this involve a slightly different form of interpretation of the passage's context from that in the previous question. People's characters can emerge from various aspects of a text:
- what people think
- the tone in which they think it
- what people say
- the tone in which they say it
- what people do.

To note simply what people think, say and do would, however, only gain enough marks for one of the lowest GCSE grades: in every case, you need to look at the connotations of words *and actions* in terms of character. In other words, you need to ask yourself, "What sort of person would think/say/do that?" You can find more about characterisation in the next chapter.

> *Answer*
> Jane is a nervous, shy child: we can see this from her sitting back and hiding her face, her breaking her slate, her feeling rooted to the spot, and her shaking or "palsy". She has strength of feeling, however: the incident awakens her "fury". This is followed by courage not to "shirk" the trial, but to put up with or "sustain" it.

Answering the Questions

This answer depends on good descriptive words to name different aspects of Jane's character: *nervous*, *shy*, *strength of feeling*, *courage*. More is said about character-terms in the next chapter. In this answer the quotations have been reduced to one key word in each case: this is a very economical way of making a point, but depends on your knowing exactly which word you are responding to.

Q4. This is a small incident, but may still seem quite dramatic to you. Write down what you think might give it this dramatic quality.

Drama in plot is not necessarily created by big, heroic events: it occurs wherever there is a conflict in which you the reader are interested to take sides. This question is more general in nature than the other three, and requires brief reference to be made to a large number of points. There is more about the nature of drama in the next chapter.

ACTIONS AS WELL AS WORDS PLAY A PART IN THE DRAMA.

Answering the Questions

Answer
The drama in this passage comes from the conflict between Jane and Mr. Brocklehurst. We sympathise with Jane because she is telling us of the ordeal, and because she is young and frightened, as we see from her cowering and trembling, for instance. Her emotions, which are those of a frightened child, and her courage make us feel for her, as does Miss Temple's being on her side. Brocklehurst's pompous coldness and his willingness to blame Jane make us dislike him for threatening her. His speeches in the passage are aggressive in tone, whether short exclamations like "A careless girl!" or longer, moralistic condemnations of Jane. The unpleasantness of her position is brought out by the fact that she has to remain silent, and can only react in her thoughts.

Actions as well as words play a part in the drama of this passage: the crashing of the slate starts the scene with a shock, and the conflict is translated into action when Brocklehurst forces Jane to come out in front of the class and stand on a "very high" stool.

The main sources of drama in a plot – conflict and danger – are covered in this answer, as well as the ways in which it can be presented, through speeches, thoughts and actions.
- Make points in your answers by using *brief* quotations from the passage.
- Explain what the passage suggests as well as what it says on the surface.
- Consider the meanings of actions as well as of words.

2 Understanding Plays, Novels and Short Stories

Getting the Full Picture

Exercises like those described in the last chapter check how well you understand the detail of prose passages, and give you a chance to comment on their authors' styles. But when you come to read a whole story, novel or play, you need another set of skills to develop an understanding of the story as a whole and a grasp of what it adds up to – the ideas and impressions it leaves on its readers.

If you ask a child what a story is about, he or she will reply in a manner something like this: "Well, there was this beautiful princess, you see, and the wicked witch was jealous of her and put her to sleep for a hundred years. And she lay in the palace all asleep, until . . ." Simply retelling a story, however, will not gain many marks at GCSE level. There are other, more revealing ways of thinking about a story, and it is these that the examination is concerned with.

You need to ask why people enjoy reading novels or stories or watching plays. Arguably, we enjoy them because they enable us to imagine life from the points of view of other people – that is, of the *characters* in the story, as well as of its author. We are always trying to make sense of life, and stories stimulate our imagination as we try to do so. If a story makes us laugh or feel pity or fear, our experience of life has been extended in our imagination. In other words, our interest in stories is a development of our interest in people, and one way in which we can study stories is to concentrate on the characters in them.

The characters in any form of story are normally set against a *background*: they are supposed to live in a particular time and place, and occupy a given position in *society*. Often these factors are important: the *Jane Eyre* scene used in Chapter 1 could only have happened in nineteenth-century England, and that part of the book can be seen as a criticism of nineteenth-century society. In such cases it is valuable to extend our study of individual characters to their background and society.

Stories do not necessarily reflect life realistically, of course, but they each reflect human life in some way. In animal stories, the animals have human characteristics. In fantasy and science fiction, the characters, creatures and situations may also reflect the author's views of life or ideas about humanity's desires or fears. Embedded in any story or play are the author's ideas about what life is like, and it is usually possible to study these. We often refer to the ideas that come up in a book as its *themes*.

One of the skills we can look for in an author is the construction of a good *plot*. A plot can be judged not only on whether it keeps us interested, but also on whether it provides incidents that all help us to imagine the characters and understand the themes.

The five approaches just mentioned – *characters*, *background*, *society*, *themes* and *plot* – form the basis of the rest of this chapter. If you are studying a book for any examination at the end of the course, you should make five sets of revision notes, one on each of the topics. Later we shall see how they come up in many of the essays set for GCSE assessments and examinations.

- Stories and plays help us imagine life as it is, and how we might like it to be or fear that it could be.
- Stories and plays are based round characters and relationships, settings and incidents.
- Stories and plays often express their authors' ideas about life, in their themes.
- Plots function by interesting us in the characters and providing incidents that help us understand themes.
- *Don't* just summarise the story-line of a book in an essay; analyse the book in terms of the above ideas.

Character

WE REACT INSTANTLY TO THE IMPRESSIONS WE GAIN OF OTHER PEOPLE'S CHARACTERS.

When we meet someone in real life, we react instantly to the impression we have gained of his or her character. Such a first impression might be gained from, amongst other things, the person's clothes, hair-style, facial expression, or the person's way of standing, walking or talking. Later we would modify our opinion, taking into consideration what the person has said and done whilst we have known him or her. We would probably try to spot patterns in his or her behaviour and generalise from them: for instance, if the person were always on the move, talked loudly, laughed and sang a lot, and occasionally lapsed into panic, we would probably decide that these were signs of excitement, and we might wish to say that he or she had an excitable character or temperament. Of course, excitability would be only one aspect of that person's character: he or she might also be intelligent or stupid, good-tempered or bad-tempered and so on. We can call each of these aspects a character *trait*, and it is helpful to be able to name traits with a suitable noun or adjective.

Methods of Characterisation

It is just the same with characters in plays and stories. The evidence from which we can arrive at a judgement on a person's character-traits can come in several forms:
- description of the person
- opinions expressed by the story-teller
- the person's actions
- the person's words
- the person's thoughts

In a novel or story, when we first come across a character, he or she is often described by the story-teller, and we form a first impression from this. Occasionally the story-teller will pass an opinion about a character, which also helps us. Note that you don't have to agree with this opinion, especially if the story-teller is also a character in the story. In *The Great Gatsby* by F. Scott Fitzgerald, the hero is introduced as follows:

> He smiled understandingly – much more than understandingly. It was one of those rare smiles with a quality of eternal reassurance in it, that you may come across four or five times in life... Precisely at that point it vanished – and I was looking at an elegant young rough-neck, a year or two over thirty.

Here, the author's comments seem contradictory: is Gatsby wise, sincere, or a "young rough-neck"? When there are conflicts of evidence, like this, you should choose which interpretation best fits the facts of the whole story and work out why the author has put in the misleading words. The effect is to make you judge the characters for yourself. (Occasionally an author will put in a comment that is obviously the opposite of what he or she means: this technique is known as *verbal irony*.)

In plays, of course, we find little description or comment. Some can be given by other characters, however, and a little can be given in stage directions, which are usually worth noting.

Characters' actions come into both stories and plays, and are always significant. In *The Great Gatsby*, the hero gets the story-teller to arrange for him to meet the woman he loves: despite his being rich and successful, he is not confident enough to do this himself. This helps us understand one of the ways he is putting on pretences throughout his life.

Probably the most important source of characterisation, however, is a person's words: indeed, in a play they are almost all we have to go on. We can think about not only what a character says, but also how he or she says it. The style of speech will affect the way we feel about it, and the

Character

judgements we make on the speaker. In Arthur Miller's play, *Death of a Salesman*, Willy Loman describes to his son his formula for success:

> "The man who makes an appearance in the business world, the man who creates personal interest, is the man who gets ahead. Be liked and you will never want. You take me, for instance. I never have to wait in line to see a buyer. 'Willy Loman is here!' That's all they have to know, and I go right through."

We can spot the boasting tone in these words, and wonder if they are really true.

Characters' thoughts are available to us in novels and stories, and they help us imagine the thinkers in much the same way as their speeches. They can, indeed, reveal more, since what people say is partly governed by their relationship with the people to whom they are speaking, whilst thoughts are completely candid. In plays, we can be shown characters' thoughts in two different ways. Older plays, including those by Shakespeare, contain long speeches made by characters when they are left alone on the stage: this type of speech is called a *soliloquy*, and normally it is used to tell us what a character is thinking.

The other way of indicating a thought in a play is the *aside*, a short remark made by a character which some or all of the characters on stage do not hear. This happens in Bill Naughton's *Spring and Port Wine*, when Harold Crompton feels that his overbearing father has been selfish in spending a great deal of money on a hand-made overcoat, whilst keeping his wife short of housekeeping money. He dare not say what he thinks out loud, so he adds comments which his father, Rafe, cannot hear, but which his brother and sister are aware of.

> RAFE: No fussing now. Anybody'ud think you'd never seen a new topcoat.
> HAROLD (*aside*): We haven't – not one as cost that much.
> DAISY: . . . That looks grand, Dad.
> WILFRED: It's a good fit, eh, Harold?
> HAROLD: Aye. (*Aside.*) It fits where it touches.

Terms for Character Traits

It is obviously important to have a good vocabulary for describing aspects of characters. The following list contains many useful terms, but there are a great many more available. Adjectives are given here, but in most cases nouns can be formed from them – for instance, the trait that makes someone *hypocritical* would be *hypocrisy*.

active	imaginative	selfless
adventurous	immature	sensual
aggressive	impulsive	sentimental
ambitious	insincere	sincere
angry	intellectual	sociable
balanced	intelligent	solitary
conscientious	lazy	strait-laced
courageous	loving	stupid
cowardly	mature	superstitious
dishonest	mean	sympathetic
educated	naïve	taciturn
emotional	open-minded	tactful
excitable	passionate	tactless
forthright	peaceful	talkative
friendly	placid	temperamental
generous	practical	truthful
hateful	prejudiced	unambitious
honest	relaxed	unbalanced
humorous	religious	vain
hypocritical	romantic	virtuous
ignorant	selfish	witty

Look through this list and make sure that you understand each word. Use a dictionary if necessary.

Assessing a Character

Once you have decided what traits a character has, you need to work out your attitude to the person thus created. Here are some topics you should consider.

1. *Is the character believable?* Characters are more than simple collections of traits: the traits must fit together in a credible way. Although, as we have seen, there seems to be a contradiction between Gatsby's confident, warm smile, and the coolness with which he could turn it off, by the end of the novel we can understand that Gatsby has based his whole career on using the ugly side of life to make money, for him to act out his dreams: this lack of integrity is at the centre of his life, and everything he does is tainted by it.

2. *Does the character develop?* The main characters in stories and plays usually change as a result of the things that happen to them. They may learn about life or about themselves, or become better or worse people. In *Wuthering Heights* by Emily Brontë, Heathcliff always has a tendency towards ill-temperedness, but it is not until he has been humiliated by Hindley and abandoned by Cathy that he becomes obsessed with vengeance. It is credible that he should do so, and this emphasises one of the book's themes— that there is both good and evil in everybody.

3. *Does the character appeal to you?* What makes the character interesting? What makes you feel for (or against) him or her? Heathcliff, for instance, is interesting because he is always strong-willed, passionate and unconventional.

4. *Is the character meaningful?* How does the character relate to the book's themes and provide us with food for thought? We have seen how Willy Loman's advice to his son shows the shoddiness of his own ideals. This can be compared with the behaviour of other characters in the play, and we may come to believe that Miller is showing us the extent to which insincerity is, he believes, built into the American way of life.

- Develop a good vocabulary for character-traits.
- Develop the habit of trying to spot and name character-traits.
- Assess whether characters hang together well and develop realistically.
- Relate characters to the story's themes.

Relationships

Characters in stories and plays rarely exist on their own; in fact, plots usually depend on the effect of the characters on each other. Stories can deal with a person's learning to cope with the natural world: Daniel Defoe's *Robinson Crusoe* starts this way. So, too, does the modern novel *Z for Zachariah* by Robert C. O'Brien, in which the heroine at first believes herself to be the only person left alive after a nuclear disaster. Her story gains greatly in interest, however, when a stranger arrives, who appears at first to be a friend and later to be an enemy. The themes of many stories are about how we relate to one another: *Z for Zachariah* shows how little can be achieved if two people do not trust each other.

Relationships can be judged from the same signs as characters – descriptions, comments, and characters' thoughts, words and deeds. Like characters, relationships develop with time: at first the heroine in *Z for Zachariah* is open and friendly with the stranger, but later distrusts him because he tries to control her possessively. In thinking about relationships we need to:

- describe their quality (for instance, they may be friendly, close, truthful or distrustful, distant, unfriendly);
- describe why they are like this (what the causes are in people's characters and circumstances);
- describe how and why they change.

We can evaluate relationships in the same way as characters. Questions to ask about a relationship include:

Is it credible? If so, why?

Is it interesting?

What feelings do you have about it?
Is it meaningful in terms of the book's themes?
- Stories usually depend on relationships.
- Relationships are caused by characters and circumstances.
- The development of relationships often illustrates a book's themes.

Settings

Physical Background

The background to the action of a story can be important in many ways. The time and place of a story – even the weather at the time – can cause events to take place. *Z for Zachariah* could only take place after a nuclear war, and Robinson Crusoe would not have survived if he had not landed on a fertile tropical island. In each case, the setting of the story also provides many of the problems that the characters have to overcome, and contributes to the story's atmosphere. In some cases, of course, the background is important only in order to create a mood, but normally it will contribute to the plot as well.

Settings

We can study the physical background to a story by analysing descriptions of it and references to it. The following are fruitful questions to ask:
- Does the setting affect the characters in any way?
- Does it set a mood or tone for the story?
- Does it set (or solve) any problems for the character?
- Does it illustrate the story or play's theme?

Social Background

In many stories and some plays there are numerous minor characters who contribute little directly to the plot, but who add greatly to the book's interest: they may be intriguing, funny or sinister in their own right. The farm-hands in Thomas Hardy's *Far from the Madding Crowd* come to mind. We witness them gossiping on several occasions and come to realise that they represent a whole social class of people, the uneducated workers, and that these contrast with the hero and heroine, who are educated and quicker-minded. It is clear that Hardy is saying something about the nature of Victorian society here, and the value of education. In *To Kill a Mockingbird*, Harper Lee shows us many of the black and white inhabitants of Maycomb, Alabama, in America's Deep South; and we realise that something is being said about their attitudes to one another – especially about their prejudices.

Not all stories have a well-developed social background; and plays, which generally have few characters, have a well-developed social background even less often than stories. Some plays do, however, tell the story of a whole community by settling on several individuals or families to carry the plot, as in Arthur Miller's *The Crucible* or Ronald Eyre's *The Roses of Eyam*. In both of these the community's leaders are surrounded by families representative of the whole community. On the other hand, in Harold Brighouse's *Hobson's Choice*, a play about Victorian values, there are comparatively few characters, but social values are openly discussed:

> "I'm British middle class and proud of it. I stand for common-sense and sincerity. You're affected, which is bad sense and insincerity . . . You forget the majesty of trade and unparalleled virtues of the British Constitution which are all based on the sanity of the middle classes, combined with the diligence of the working-classes."

These values are in fact central to the play, but to understand fully what is going on when they are mentioned, you have to take them in context, and ask *who* is mentioning them, and *why*. Henry Horatio Hobson is telling his daughters off for their supposedly light-headed behaviour, when it is actually his daughter Maggie who most embodies the values he is talking about: he himself is a worthless drunkard. Thus we can see that the play not only includes discussion of Victorian values, it represents them – and their opposite – in the lives of its characters.

In all these plays, as well as many novels and stories, society is part of the subject of the piece, which is about more than merely the individual characters' actions.

Religion

Often, characters' beliefs are important in a story: *The Crucible*, for instance, is about witchcraft, and Christian people's reactions to it. Some of the characters seem to be so obsessed with evil that they see it whether it is there or not, perhaps because of their own sense of guilt. One of the play's themes is about knowing what the world is really like, and the story shows that if our attitudes are wrong, seriously held beliefs can on occasion hide the truth rather than reveal it.

Questions to ask about the background and setting of stories:
- Do nature, time or place play an active part in the text you are dealing with?
- Do the characters represent one or more social classes?
- Is the story influenced by the characters' religions or ideals?
- Are any of the story's themes about the nature of society?

Themes

All writers have beliefs about life, society and the world; and whether consciously or not, these beliefs are expressed in what they write. If we look at a text and spot which ideas and beliefs lie behind it, we can come close to saying what it is about at the deepest level.

Occasionally a story-teller will make a comment about life; more often, the story-teller will put it into the mouth of one of the characters. If this comment comes in a position of great emphasis – at the beginning or end of a chapter, or close to an important event – we should ask ourselves if it reveals something of the author's thinking about the story. In *To Kill a Mockingbird*, Atticus Finch tells his daughter Scout his views on prejudice:

> "This case, Tom Robinson's case, is something that goes to the essence of a man's conscience – Scout, I couldn't go to church and worship God if I didn't try to help that man."

Themes

We know that prejudice causes many of the story's events, from the accusation of rape made against the negro Tom Robinson, to the children's fear of the mysterious Boo Radley. Because we can make this link between a comment and several events in the story, we can say that the nature of prejudice is one of the themes of *To Kill a Mockingbird*. The fact that the comment and the story back each other up clinches the matter.

Not all comments work as simply as this, however. In stories, authors' comments may go against the evidence of the plot and be meant ironically. In John Galsworthy's play, *Strife*, employers and trades unionists have opposite interpretations of what is going on.

> ROBERTS: There's not one sentence of writing on that paper that we can do without . . . Not one single sentence. All those demands are fair. We have not asked anything that we are not entitled to ask. What I said in London, I say again now: there is not anything on that piece of paper that a just man should not ask, and a just man give. [*A pause.*]
> ANTHONY: There is not one single demand on this paper that we will grant.

Both sides cannot be right: one, or both, must be wrong. It is necessary to see which explanation best fits what is going on in the play in order to fix on Galsworthy's theme.

Sometimes an author will make no comment on the story, but a theme can still be seen through the story's patterning. In *Billy Liar* by Keith Waterhouse there are few comments on the character and life of the main character, Billy Fisher. In the course of the novel, however, he constantly gets into scrapes due to his inability to face up to reality: nothing is quite real for him. For example, he is engaged to two girls simultaneously (with only one ring), whilst he is more in love with a third. When she invites him to leave home and go to London with her, however, he is too frightened to do so. It is the repetition of a pattern of behaviour which tells us that Waterhouse has something to say here: facing reality and making choices are part of growing up.

The repetition in *Billy Liar* is built round the actions of one character, but sometimes you will see more than one character falling into a pattern and this will also enable you to detect a theme. Often, characters are contrasted, such as Sergeant Troy and Gabriel Oak in Hardy's *Far from the Madding Crowd*. Troy is flashy, handsome, glamorous and irresponsible, whilst Oak is plodding, plain, workaday but reliable. Each lives with the consequences of his own character, and in reading the story we become conscious of a theme which shows how preferable in a man is steady reliability to mere glamour.

Plot

- Themes emerge from story-tellers' comments, characters' comments, the patterns of thoughts and happenings in a story.

Plot

> THIS BOOK HAS A REALLY EXPLOSIVE PLOT!

(GUY FAWKES)

A story's plot is its story-line, the series of events which takes place. The word *plot*, however, suggests careful planning, in order to achieve an end, and it needs to be said that the best stories do not just simply happen: they are thought out in order to fulfil certain purposes.

The series of events in a story is one of its main sources of interest. It helps if the events are surprising, as this entertains the reader, but a writer has to strike a balance between ingeniousness and naturalness. In most plots we can expect the incidents to be caused naturally either by the characters to whom they happen or by factors within their environment; these factors can be due to society (like the treatment of Jane Eyre at school) or to nature (as in the loss of Antonio's ships at sea in *The Merchant of Venice*). It is always worth commenting on whenever an event combines both naturalness and surprise for the reader.

In some cases we can tolerate plots happening which are not natural: if the story is taking place in a fantasy world, as in Tolkien's *The Lord of the Rings*, we can allow for supernatural happenings, especially if they perform some of the other plot functions mentioned below. Another sort of fantasy occurs in Shakespeare's comedies, where characters often disguise themselves and get up to other tricks that would not be possible in the real world: an example is Bassanio's sweetheart Portia, who passes herself off as a male lawyer in *The Merchant of Venice*. This adds

Plot

to the play's sense of fun, but also contributes to its meaningfulness. Probably the most unconvincing type of plotting is the multiple coincidence, as when in Hardy's *The Return of the Native* Clym's mother arrives at his cottage while he is asleep and his wife cannot open the door because a former lover of hers is present. On top of this, when the mother returns home she is bitten by an adder, and dies believing that her son has had her spurned from the door. For most readers, this long series of pieces of ill-luck is just too much!

The basis of any plot lies in a problem which the characters experience. In *Jane Eyre* it is "Will Jane find a relationship that fulfils her?" Most of the incidents in the book are to do with the amount of frustration or fulfilment she feels when she has to deal with the other characters, from her cold, self-righteous aunt, through Mr. Brocklehurst to the oh-so-temptingly masculine but slightly shady hero, Mr. Rochester. The problem behind this plot is an interesting one, because it arises both from Jane's shy yet passionate character and from her social background as an orphan. Thus, the events of the plot spring from and illuminate her character; they also illuminate the book's themes, which are about love and fulfilment.

The most meaningful things a plot event can do are to display a character, relationship or situation to us, and help us think about a story's theme: if an event does all this, we can often pass over some unnaturalness. Thus, when in *The Merchant of Venice* Portia dresses as a man, it enables her to make an impassioned speech about love and "the quality of mercy"; since the play is about mercy and love, the unnatural plotting can be expected.

A plot which seizes our interest and confronts us with the unexpected will make us wish to continue reading the story or watching the play. In doing so, it will provide us either with suspense or with comedy – sometimes with both. *Suspense* and *drama* arise from the problems characters experience in a story. In a good plot, many things happen to delay the solution of the problems, and each of these will contribute to the plot's suspense. Suspense and drama also depend on our identifying imaginatively with some of the characters in the plot – feeling for and with them, and wanting them to succeed in achieving a happy ending.

Comedy, the other source of pleasure which keeps us reading or watching, depends more on our standing outside the characters in the book or play. We laugh when they say or do something that we know to be foolish: if suspense makes us share fictional characters' fears, comedy makes us feel happy and safe. It is worth commenting on factors which make a scene tense or a book comic.

Irony. Often, when reading or seeing a story for the first time, you get a sense that a character is being foolish – that he or she is doing or saying things which will later prove to be wrong.

In Jane Austen's *Northanger Abbey*, the heroine, Catherine Morland, believes for much of the novel that the house named in the title holds terrible secrets, and that its owner has a hidden, evil side. It is obvious to the reader that she is wrong and is making a fool of herself because of having read too many horror novels. This sense of her folly is of course increased on second and further readings: it is a form of *dramatic irony*, the sense that a character's folly will rebound on him or her later in the plot. According to the tone of the book or play, such ironies can also be called *comic* (as here) or *tragic*. An example of the latter is the feeling we get when Macbeth starts to believe the three witches: he wants to believe that they are promising him the crown for his own good, whilst we can see that they are luring him to destruction.

Surprisingly, for all their apparently infinite variety, plots mostly have the same basic shape. The first part of a plot, which we can call the *exposition*, enables you to get to know the characters, their background, and the problem that sets the story going. This may overlap slightly with the *development*, in which the characters take action to solve their problem – by, for instance, seeking a lover, looking for a murderer, leaving home, and so on. In the first part of the development, if the story is to have a happy ending, the characters will usually meet a series of unpleasant situations, so that we doubt whether they will eventually succeed. One event will provoke a crisis or period of extreme tension, after which our heroes and/or heroines begin to win through. In tragic plots the hero or heroine may appear to succeed at first, but the crisis will start a series of events which defeat him or her. Finally, the plot reaches a *resolution*, a happy solution to the problems or a tragic outcome. Given any scene from a set book, you should be able to show just where it falls in this scheme of things, and what factors within it make it expose or develop character, background and plot, or resolve the plot's problems.

- Plot is the organisation of events to intrigue and entertain.
- Plots may be realistic or fantastic.
- You should be able to show how each major scene contributes to the plot's exposition, development or resolution.

Making Notes

The quantity of notes you will need to make depends on how you are being assessed on a text. As you are being taught a text, you should make rough notes about all the approaches mentioned in this chapter, as and when they come up. You can sometimes make enough notes by writing in the margin of the book you are studying (*only* if it is your own copy), but you will find a separate notebook is quicker to use when you come to plan essays or when you revise.

If you are being assessed on a book by coursework only, all you need do in addition to the above is use your rough notes to plan out your essays and exercises. If, on the other hand, you are going to sit an examination at the end of the course, you will need revision notes. Some of these you will no doubt have made in class, and your essays may stand in for them on some topics; others you will need to make from your rough notes as you revise.

Plays, Films and Videos

Students often ask whether they should make an effort to go to a performance of a set play, or to see a film or video based on a set novel. The answer to the first of these is yes, since watching a stage production of a play will bring it alive in a way no mere reading can. But films and videos, whether based on plays, novels or short stories, can be misleading, and should be approached with caution. In any case, watching a performance should be additional to, and not in place of, a thorough reading of the set text.

Watching Plays

For many students, a trip to watch a GCSE set play is the first time they have ever set foot in a theatre – or certainly the first time they have gone to watch anything other than a pantomime or a pop concert. Often they are amazed at how gripping an experience it can be to watch live actors – much more involving in many ways than watching them on film or television – so that for this experience alone the trip to the theatre is worth while. Good actors will have studied the play in depth themselves, and will have arrived at their own conclusions about its characters, relationships, plot and so on. They will have considered how to bring these things out on stage, and, if they are performing well, will make the play much clearer and more memorable for you.

At the same time as enjoying a production, however, you may decide that some aspects are not as you expected them: a character may not come over just as you thought, or the plot may run slower or faster than you expected. Modern designers can be adventurous with their sets, and the setting of the play may surprise you. All this is fair enough, since the actors are only putting over their interpretation of the play, which is one of many interpretations, another of them being yours. You may be right, and they may be wrong, or vice versa; or both interpretations may be possible. Thus, watching a production of a play can open your eyes to the play's possibilities and lead to good class-room discussion. In particular, you will learn how a playwright can give actors opportunities in the script for emotional moments, characterisation and actions which affect the audience's appreciation of a play. Often, comments which show that you have watched a performance and thought about it will obtain for you higher marks than ones based on just reading a play.

Films and Videos

Films and videos of plays need treating with more caution than stage performances, since film and television directors often *adapt* plays for the screen. Because films and videos can show outdoor scenes and can cope with many more scene changes than a stage production, quite a number of directors seem to think that they *must* have these features in them. At best, a film may have extra scenes in it, which are written in the same style as the original play, and which join the main scenes together: this is true, for example, of the 1950's film of *Hobson's Choice*, a play often set for GCSE. After watching the film, you could discuss it as if it were a stage production, but take care to check which scenes are in the play script and which are not. For a coursework exercise you might even write an essay on the differences between the play and the film; but if you were trying to revise the play for an exam, all these differences might simply confuse you, and you would be better off with the text alone. Some film versions of plays totally swamp the original script in new additions and are useless as revision material. Whenever the opportunity to watch a film or video of a set text comes up, discuss it with your teacher.

Film and video versions of novels and stories are even more of a problem. When an author writes a story, he or she tries to set down on the page everything that you will need in order to follow and understand the story: you should not need a performance to help you do this. To make films, novels have to be cut down drastically: whole sections of the plot will be left out, and several characters may go missing. To base your ideas of a novel on a film can therefore be seriously misleading, and watching one is advisable only in two types of circumstance:

1. if a novel completely baffles you, in which case you may gain some basic ideas about it from the film;
2. if you are really interested in films and want to write about the differences between the film and the book.

- Stage performances of plays can bring them really alive.
- Film and video adaptations of novels can be confusing or misleading.
- Discuss with your teacher any production you have seen.

3 Writing About Plays, Novels and Short Stories

You can have your head bursting with ideas about the books you have read; but, unless you can write about them in a way that your examiner or assessor will accept, you will not get a good GCSE grade. Reading this chapter should help you to think out, plan, research and write the sorts of answers that receive high grades.

Forms of Assessment

Just how you approach a question will depend on whether you are doing it as part of your coursework, or whether you are doing it for an examination. As we have seen, there are different types of exam: in some you can use your set books, whilst in others you have to work from memory. Nevertheless the principles of writing good answers are always the same: basically, there are just two types of exercise – passages with short questions, and essays.

Passages with Questions

Normally, this type of exercise looks like a comprehension or an unseen appreciation exercise. In open-book examinations or classwork, however, the passage may not be reprinted: you will simply be told in what scene or chapter (and what paragraphs of that chapter) you can find it. The main difference between this sort of exercise and an unseen appreciation is that the questions will assume you do have knowledge of the text as a whole: for example, in a question about character you may need to have a clear picture of the character as he or she appears throughout the book, not just in the selected passage. In a question about plot, you will probably need to be able to refer to events in other parts of the story.

EVEN IN OPEN-BOOK EXAMS YOU NEED TO KNOW THE BOOK THOROUGHLY.

Essays

The basic method of testing your knowledge of English Literature remains the essay. The subjects most often set are related to the areas of interest studied in the last chapter – character, relationships, theme and plot – but any essay can require you to refer to more than one of these areas.

For success in the GCSE, it is very important to develop a suitable essay technique, and the first element of this is to understand the types of question that you may come across. There are various ways of setting essay questions. In each case, a careful consideration of exactly what the question is asking will pay off well.

1. *Title.* The most obvious way of setting an exercise is to give you a title that tells you what to write about – for example:

<u>Pride and Prejudice</u> *What makes Elizabeth Bennet an interesting and amusing heroine?*

Given a title like this, you need to sit and think for a while about precisely what the question is asking you. The key words are *interesting* and *amusing*: whatever events and character-traits you write about will have to be linked to these two ideas.

2. *Title with Stimulus.* Sometimes an essay title may include a quotation that is meant to set you thinking about the book in question, for instance:

<u>Z for Zachariah</u> *"This book is not mainly about nuclear war. Its real theme is the loss of innocence." What are your views on this subject? Write an essay either supporting or criticising the statement.*

Here you have two elements to think about before you begin writing – the quotation and the instructions that follow it. Make sure you have understood *both*. Look for the main ideas in the quotation – here they are nuclear war and the loss of innocence – and try to decide what they mean. Then look at the instructions and make sure you have got them clear in your mind: for example, here you are being asked to write *for* or *against* the quotation, not on both sides.

3. *Title with Essay-Structure.* Either of the above types of title can be combined with a list of ideas for you to consider in your essay:

<u>Macbeth</u> *What do you think are the main causes of Macbeth's downfall? Write about* three *of the following topics:*

 Macbeth's character
 The Three Witches
 Lady Macbeth
 Macduff

This type of exercise is very helpful because it reminds you that literature essays have to be planned out topic by topic, and should not simply retell the story. Make sure you know how many of the suggested topics you have to cover, and whether you are expected to add topics of your own.

4. *Title with Passage.* Either type of essay question can also be combined with a passage from a set text, like this:

<u>A Taste of Honey</u> *Reread Act I Scene 1 from the beginning up to Helen's singing "I'd give the song birds to the wild wood." Show how this informs the audience about the characters of Helen and Jo, and their problems.*

Notice that this title asks you about the selected passage in relation to the rest of the play: you need to know about how the characters behave later in order to say whether you have got a good picture of them from the passage.

5. *Titles Involving Writing in Roles.* Sometimes you will be given the option of writing as if you were a character in a set text:

Spring and Port Wine *Imagine Rafe some days later looking back at the events of the play. What would he now think of the behaviour of himself, his wife and his children? You may write as if you were Rafe, if you wish.*

Note first that this question asks you to consider the character Rafe has become at the end of the play: you are to describe the play not as you see it, but as he would see it. Secondly, note that you do not have to write your answer in his words, though it may help to do so.

Two ways of writing in a role

As a character
I was shocked when I realised that Daisy had forced open my box: I knew that she was slightly scared.

Reporting a character
Rafe must have been shocked when he realised that Daisy had forced open his box. He obviously knew that . . .

---

6. *Titles Involving Rewriting.* A variation on role-writing is rewriting an aspect of a book or play in a different form. Writing letters from one character to another, and writing newspaper stories, are two types of this exercise. Remember that you can look to English Language books for advice on tackling the different sorts of writing: for example, you could look at the GCSE *English Grade Booster*, pages 28-66.

- In open-book exams you will need to know your text very thoroughly in order to find your way around it quickly.
- Beware of doing questions on passages simply because you do not know a text well: the questions will almost always refer outside the passage.
- Study all questions closely. Pick out:
  1. the main ideas you are asked about,
  2. what you have to write about these ideas,
  3. any viewpoint or role that you must assume.
- All essays should be structured round topics, and should not merely retell the story.
- If you write in a role, remember that what you write is more important than your style.

Worked Exercises

1. Passage with Questions

Hobson's Choice

Read the following passage and answer the questions printed under it.

(WILLIE goes to the bedroom and returns with a slate and slate pencil. The slate is covered in writing. He puts it on the table.)
MAGGIE: Off with your Sunday coat now. You don't want to make a mess of that.
(WILLIE takes coat off and gets a rag from behind the screen and brings it back to the table. He hangs his coat on a peg.)
MAGGIE: What are you doing with that mopping rag?
WILLIE: I was going to wash out what's on the slate.
MAGGIE: Let me see it first. That's what you did last night at Tubby's after I came here?
WILLIE: Yes, Maggie.
MAGGIE (*reading*): "There is always room at the top." (*She washes it out.*) Your writing's improving, Will. I'll set you a short copy for tonight, because it's getting late and we've a lot to do in the morning. (*She writes*) "Great things grow from small." Now, then, you can sit down here and copy that.
(*WILLIE takes her place at the table. MAGGIE watches a moment, then goes to the fireplace and fingers the flowers.*)
MAGGIE: I'll put these flowers of Mrs. Hepworth's behind the fire, Will. We'll not want litter in the place come working time tomorrow. (*She takes up the basin, stops, looks at Willie, who is bent over his slate, and takes a flower out, throwing the rest behind the fire and going to the bedroom with the one.*)
WILLIE (*looking up*): You're saving one.
MAGGIE (*caught in an act of sentiment and apologetically*): I thought I'd press it in my Bible for a keepsake, Will. I'm not beyond liking to be reminded of this day. (*She looks at the screen and yawns*) Lord, I'm tired. I reckon I'll leave those pots till morning. It's a slackish way of starting, but I don't get married every day.
WILLIE (*industrious at his slate*): No.
MAGGIE: I'm for my bed. You finish that copy before you come.
WILLIE: Yes, Maggie.
(*Exit MAGGIE to the bedroom, with the flower. She closes the door. WILLIE copies, repeats the letters and the words as he writes*

them slowly, finishes, then rises and rakes out the fire. He looks shyly at the bedroom door, sits and takes his boots off. He rises, boots in his hand, moves towards the door, hesitates, and turns back, puts the boots down at the door, then returns to the table and takes off his collar. Then hesitates again, finally makes up his mind, puts out the light, and lies down on the sofa with occasional glances at the bedroom door. At first he faces the fire. He is uncomfortable. He turns over and faces the door.

In a minute MAGGIE opens the bedroom door. She has a candle and is in a plain calico night-dress. She comes to WILLIE, shines the light on him, takes him by the ear, and returns with him to the bedroom.)

1. What aspects of Maggie's character are shown in this scene? Which of them might the audience find surprising?
2. How does this scene mark a stage in Willie Mossop's development during the play?
3. What is the significance of the following in the scene?
    (a) the slate and slate pencil;
    (b) what Maggie and Willie write on the slate;
    (c) the flowers;
    (d) the washing-up which is left undone.
4. What might the effect of the silent scene (described in the last stage directions) be on the audience at a performance of the play?

Comments on the Questions

You will notice a general similarity between this exercise and the unseen appreciation passage in Chapter 1. There are two main differences, however:

(i) The questions all assume that you know the rest of the play. To be surprised at any of Maggie's characteristics, you must have come to the scene with some expectations from earlier in the plot; to be aware of a stage in Willie's development, you have to know about his life before and after the scene.

(ii) The questions relate not only to the words of the text, but also, since this is a play, to the props and actions that the audience see. Notice how it would be a definite advantage, when doing this exercise, to have actually seen a performance of the play.

Worked Exercises

Answering the Questions

Q1. *What aspects of Maggie's character are shown in this scene? Which of them might the audience find surprising?*

First ask yourself how many things this question is asking you. It has two aspects: (a) you can gain marks by mentioning simple character-points about Maggie; and (b) you need to say which of these points are surprising. You can start by approaching each aspect separately. Without any knowledge of the play, you should be able to pick out several aspects of Maggie's character from her words and actions. Perhaps you should try to do this now, before reading the following answer.

> *Answer*
> Maggie's ambitious nature comes over from the slogans she is teaching Willie – and from the fact that she is teaching him to write at all. She is almost domineering in her control over him, setting him a task before bedtime on their wedding night, and leading him off to bed by the ear. She displays a very practical, down-to-earth attitude by throwing away the flowers: this seems quite a cold thing to do, until she keeps one to press. Her "plain calico night-dress" is in keeping with this practicality. Perhaps she has a warm nature which she normally suppresses. Her human side also comes out when she leaves the washing-up till morning . . .

So far so good: as usual the answer makes its points and illustrates them with quotations or with references to what happens. Without further knowledge of the play, however, you would have to guess at what might be surprising about Maggie's character. For instance, throwing away the flowers appears to be an unusual act, and for a Victorian lady to drag her man off to bed seems quite extraordinary. In fact, if you had read the whole of the play you would know that Maggie is *always* down-to-earth and unconventional, and delights in taking the lead and letting men follow. To someone who knows Maggie, the moment of tenderness over the flower is at least as surprising as her tough-seeming actions. Therefore a good answer to the second part of the question would run like this, putting Maggie's actions into the context of her character as it is shown in the rest of the play:

> . . . Her rough, *almost* heartless attitude to the flowers is sufficiently cool to be a surprise, as is the coolness with which she leads Willie off to bed. She is probably teasing him, since her manner to him has been one of teasing since she decided to propose to him. For instance, she tells him he is a "business

> proposition" even though it is clear that she does love him. Her moment of warmth about the flowers is almost as surprising to someone who has observed her. She rarely shows such warmth in the play. Perhaps she is protecting her tender aspects when she is teasing him.

Notice how considering her actions in context has led to a further realisation about her character – the possibility that she is protecting herself. Without knowing the rest of the play you could not safely reach this conclusion. You need a specific piece of background information – that she is plain and considered an "old maid" – to be sure of it.

Q2. *How does this scene mark a stage in Willie Mossop's development during the play?*

This question has only one section to it: everything you write must refer to Willie Mossop's development. You will need to write about his character, but only if you can see how it changes. Here, once again, you should be able to find some things to say about Willie's character. He is clearly a willing learner, and perhaps a little submissive, with his "Yes, Maggie." He notices Maggie's actions, as when he sees her saving a flower, and is clearly very shy. *None of this gives us a stage in his development, however:* to make any points that will gain marks you need to know several background facts about him: (a) he has been considered stupid by other people; (b) he never thought about bettering himself until Maggie persuaded him; (c) he has always been easily led and shy; BUT (d) he is really clever in some ways – he is a superb craftsman; and (e) within a year he will be beginning to be well off, and have a great deal more self-confidence, owing to Maggie. A good answer, therefore, would be about the stage Willie has reached in this transformation process.

> *Answer*
> Willie here shows that he is still easily led by Maggie, doing lessons at her bidding even on his wedding night, just as he let himself be pushed into marrying her. Later he will be able to stand up to her over the name of the business when they take over her father's shop. In the month he has known Maggie, he has learned to write and is proving to himself that he does not have a slow mind; this will be adding to his self-confidence. He is still shy, however, as he was in front of Mrs. Hepworth, and when Maggie proposed to him; possibly he is frightened of his new wife when he will not go into the bedroom. In a year's time, at the play's end, he will be confident

> enough to face up to Maggie and her father at the same time over the question of the ownership of the Hobson business.

Everything in this answer is balanced between past and present; the one thing that could not be fitted into a picture of Willie's growth-process – the way in which he notices Maggie – has been left out.

Q3. *What is the significance of the following in the scene?*
  (a) the slate and slate pencil;
  (b) what Maggie and Willie write on the slate;
  (c) the flowers;
  (d) the washing-up which is left undone.

Here, you are being asked about "significance", or meaning. What sorts of meaning could this be?
  1. *Thematic*: parts of the scene will probably emphasise one of the play's main themes or ideas.
  2. *Character*: you could show how the aspect you are looking at conveys character or relationships.
  3. *Development*: you could look for meanings which contribute to the development of characters or the plot.
  4. *Contextual*: meanings may help you understand the historical, social or other type of background.

Significance means slightly more than *meaning*, however. For something to be significant it has to have *importance*. Therefore, you should be looking for meanings whose importance you can explain.

In this question, you are asked to concentrate mainly on things and actions, rather than words. This is to draw your attention again to the fact that there is more to a play than words: the actors are seen to exist, and to do things. Once more, having seen a performance would help you tackle this question. If the passage were from a novel, you might also get questions on things and actions, but you might rather expect to find questions on the words of the text, more like questions 2 and 3 of the Unseen Appreciation exercise in Chapter 1.

> *Answers*
> *(a) The slate and slate pencil*
> The author uses the slate and pencil to show us several things: Maggie's influence over Willie – she has got him restarting his life; his willingness to learn, shown by the fact that the slate and pencil have been used a great deal; Willie's intelligence, in having quickly learned to write; and his slightly childish quality, because slates were used by children learning to write.

Worked Exercises

You could say that the slate and pencil *symbolise* these things (see page 20). They could be called *visual symbols*.

> *(b) What Maggie and Willie write on the slate*
> The two slogan-like sentences are Maggie's idea, and they both put forward her Victorian determination to do well: there *is* room at the top, and she is determined to reach it with Willie. "Great things grow from small" refers to her hopes for their new business. Thus, the words reflect both her character and the social values of the time.

Here, your attention is being directed to words. The answer starts by saying that the style of the sentences is memorable: they are brief and pithy, like slogans. The answer refers outside the passage to a knowledge of Maggie's character and to a knowledge of the values of the times. This further knowledge can only come from studying the whole text.

> *(c) The flowers*
> The flowers are a visible reminder that Willie and Maggie have just got married that day. It seems a shocking action that Maggie should want to throw them away: it is as if she is wanting to throw the wedding itself away. This makes her seem too practical and no-nonsense. Yet the remaining flower, the one to be pressed, shows us that this cannot be so: "I'm not beyond liking to be reminded of this day," Maggie explains . . .

In this answer, the writer has once again treated the subject as a visual symbol, and shown how it illuminates the character most involved. The answer could be elaborated further, since Willie also notices the flowers.

> . . . Willie has noticed that she is "saving one" – perhaps this indicates that for him, too, they are meaningful . . .

This sentence shows that the writer is less sure of the line between what might be the meaning of the passage, and what might be purely a product of his or her imagination – hence the "perhaps". Another "perhaps" introduces the following comment, where again the writer's imagination is working hard, and could be seeing more in the scene than is really there.

> . . . Perhaps Maggie throws the flowers away because she would be embarrassed when customers arrived in the morning and saw this

> evidence of her wedding. She never expresses her innermost feelings in public in the play.

> **(d) The washing-up which is left undone**
> If Maggie had done the washing-up it would have shown her methodicalness and practicality, but she leaves it undone, which gives her a human touch. "It's a slackish way of starting, but I don't get married every day," she says. Once more her feelings are allowed to dictate what to do.

Here, light is shed in two ways on an action being studied, firstly through contrast, and secondly through quotation and comment. The use of contrast is interesting because the meaning of *not* doing the washing-up is made clear by examining what it would have meant if Maggie had made the *opposite* choice. This method is often useful where characters have been faced by decisions.

Q4. *What might the effect of the silent scene (described in the last stage directions) be on the audience at a performance of the play?*

This is about the effect on the audience of part of the play. "Effect" can refer to emotions which the audience might feel, or ways in which an audience-member's understanding of the play might develop.

> *Answer*
> The silent scene is primarily comic: Willie's shy look at the bedroom door, his hesitations, and his bedding-down on the sofa all show the opposite of what men are usually thought of as feeling on their wedding nights. Nor are women supposed to have to drag their men off to bed. A warm feeling mixes with the comedy because we can sympathise with Willie: Maggie is intimidating, and has partly bullied him into marrying her. There is also comedy and warmth mixed in the way she leads Willie off by the ear, treating him as a child in a teasing way. As she often does, Maggie uses an outrageous gesture to cover embarrassment.

This answer tries to explain comedy or humour in terms of a contrast. We find things comic if they are different from the way we would normally expect them to be, and if this difference is not threatening or really dangerous.

Imagine you met King Kong coming down the main street of your town or village: if you met a *real* giant gorilla the size of a bus you would probably be terrified, but if it was just a huge puppet being used by a film

Worked Exercises

company, you would probably have a giggle! It is the fact that Willie and Maggie's unexpected reactions show human weakness that makes them comic: the comedy is gentle, though, because we can also sympathise with them.

[COMIC OR DANGEROUS?]

- Decide how many parts the question has, and try to answer each one (unless a choice is given).
- Illustrate your answers with quotations and references.
- Be ready to refer outside the scene or passage printed, to other parts of the text.
- Examine characters' actions as well as the words of the text.
- In questions on plays, keep in mind what you would see on stage.

2. A Planned Essay

> Far from the Madding Crowd
> *Show how any one of Bathsheba's three relationships with men brings out both bad and good in her character.*

First stage: study the title.

Think for a moment: what is this question asking you about? Will it, for example, be necessary to write about the character of the man in question? Which of the three relationships should you choose?

This question gives you a great deal of choice, and it is clear that any one of the relationships will satisfy your assessor. You should choose the one you can write about best. This is not necessarily the one that is most important in the novel, nor the one you know most about, but the one you can most clearly think about in terms of what it shows about Bathsheba's character. You will need to write about the man's character only when it influences Bathsheba.

53

Second stage: research.

If you are writing as part of your coursework, you will next need to look through the text for places where Bathsheba and her lovers come together – that is, you will need to *conduct a search for relevant material.* You may already have chosen the relationship you are going to write about, in which case you need only research that one relationship; otherwise, you could research all three and decide later which you are going to choose.

If you made notes as you read through the book, consult them now as you skim through it. Read the relevant scenes in detail and note down the points you can make about them in a new set of notes dedicated to this essay. Try to give each note a heading and key-words to remind you instantly of *who* you are writing about, *the point* you are making, *what* happens and *where* in the book it occurs. A few lines from your notes might look like this:

Ch. 37 "The Storm – The Two Together"

p. 306 <u>Gabriel: courage, practicality, love</u> as he sees to the haystacks despite risk from lightning.

p. 307 <u>Bathsheba: practicality</u> despite her being "so distressed" about the corn.

p. 308 — <u>courage</u>: climbs the haystack despite the lightning.

p. 310 — <u>increasing maturity, decreasing vanity</u>: "Gabriel, you are kinder than I deserve." Values Gabriel's opinion; explains her trip to Bath.

p. 312 <u>Gabriel's "devotion"</u>: sees how tired she is.

There are page-references, reminders of the story, and short quotations from the text. We shall shortly see how useful short quotations can be.
Third stage: plan the essay.

When you have made a set of rough notes, you will need to think about their contents and try to put them into an order in which they can be easily written up. If possible, avoid a plan that merely allows you to retell the story or to write up your notes in story order: your assessor needs to know what *ideas* you have about the story, and you can only make these clear if you plan the essay round these ideas – one idea per paragraph.

In the case of this essay, it is asking you about the bad and good traits of Bathsheba's character. Once you have chosen the relationship you are going to study, you can organise your essay round these traits. The first stage is to take a piece of paper and give your plan a heading. Then you can make a list of the traits you are going to cover, organised into bad and good ones. You can use the list of words on page 31 to help you here.

How Bathsheba's relationship with Gabriel Oak brings out the bad and good sides of her character.

First Impressions
1. Vanity
2. Unconventionality

Bad Sides
3. Vanity
4. Emotionality and lack of self-control
5. Lack of consideration
6. Pompousness

Good Sides
7. Self-possession
8. Courage
9. Practicality
10. Maturity

Worked Exercises

Leave plenty of empty space round your plan for further notes. Each topic is numbered. Put in the numbering after you have finished the list, in case you want to alter the order in which the ideas come in your finished essay.

Now write these numbers in the appropriate places in your rough notes, so that you will quickly be able to find ideas to illustrate your essay when you come to write it.

You now need ideas for an *introduction* and a *conclusion*. These can be brief, but should not be skipped, as they will tell your assessor
  (a) at the beginning: what you think the question means, and how you are planning to answer it;
  (b) at the end: what your views add up to.
These will help your assessor to understand the points you are making, and may well bring you more marks.

In the examination room you should try to arrive at a plan like the one above before you start. You may be able to do this planning in your head, or you may wish to do it on paper. If so, write it in your answer book, label it "Plan" and, when you have finished with it, cross it out with a single diagonal line. You will not be able to research the plan: even if you are allowed to take your text into the room, there will not be enough time to look through it in detail. By the time you are in the examination room, you should have the outline of every set text in your head, and if you are allowed to use books, you should need to use them only to confirm what you already know.

Fourth stage: write the essay.

We can best study this by looking at a model answer to the question set. (The numbers in the margin would not normally appear: they refer to the notes which follow the model answer.)

Far from the Madding Crowd

Show how any one of Bathsheba's three relationships with men brings out both bad and good in her character.

① Bathsheba Everdene's relationship with Gabriel Oak is the basis of the love which eventually brings her stability, but nonetheless it still brings out both bad and good aspects of her character. Gabriel Oak is aware of her character from the start: her gazing at herself in the mirror tells him of her vanity,
② and her bold and unconventional horse-riding impresses him with her spirit.
③ Let us look at the bad and good sides in turn.

④   Bathsheba is very immature when Gabriel first proposes to her: she is impulsive and emotional, and does not consider what effect it will have on him when she runs after him, only to turn him down.

⑤   Her vanity shows in her reasons for considering his proposal: it is flattering in itself, and at a wedding she would be the centre ⑥ of attention. "People would talk about me," she says, "and I should feel triumphant and all that. But a husband – "

Later on, her vanity is offended when Gabriel shows disapproval of her love affair with Sergeant Troy. "My opinion of you is so low, that I see in your abuse the praise of discerning people!" she says, and again her emotions are out of control, so she tells Gabriel to leave her farm. Once more she is not taking into consideration Gabriel's feelings as a man who has been in love with her. Vanity turns to pompousness when shortly afterwards she has to ask him back to save her poisoned sheep: "Never will I send for him – never!" she says – but she does so, finally showing her practicality.

⑦   At other times Bathsheba does control herself and carry off difficult moments. When Gabriel asks for a job at her farm she is dignified, even if some of her thoughts are selfish: "There was room for a little pity, also for a little exultation: the former at his position, the latter at her own." She shows great courage on the ⑧ night of the storm, when she accompanies Gabriel as he fights to save the haystacks.

Bathsheba's practical nature also comes out because she, like Oak, thinks of the danger to her stacks. Similarly, it is her practicality which makes her finally send for Gabriel to save the sheep. Later she does the practical thing in letting him run the farm for her.

As time goes on, Bathsheba's judgement matures and she thinks more and more of Gabriel's maturity. She cares enough for his opinion to explain to him that when she drove off to Bath, she had intended to break off with Troy, and she is open enough to admit that her reasons for marrying Troy were ones of vanity and jealousy because "he said he had . . . seen a woman more beautiful than I". She consults Oak again over whether she should get engaged to Farmer Boldwood.

It is at this consultation that her feelings catch up with her judgement and she feels "a pang of disappointment" that Gabriel is no longer showing signs of loving her. When he tells

Worked Exercises

her of his plans to leave her farm she is disappointed, and eventually becomes sure enough of her feelings to go to him and make it clear that she would welcome it if he proposed to her again. In doing this she overcomes her vanity and humbles herself before him. Gabriel Oak is so shy that she has to insist that it is not "absurd" but only "too – s-s-soon" for them to think of marrying. Her determination coupled with her more mature judgement have enabled her to do this.

⑨ In this way the different stages of Bathsheba's relationship with Gabriel Oak illustrate her development. Always in possession of a strong and individualistic character, she has, by the end of the novel, gained some wisdom and lost some vanity.

Comment. This answer is about 700 words long. Some syllabuses mention a length of 400 or so words as being required for coursework. In practice, if you are aiming for one of the higher grades (A, B or C), you will need to regard this as a minimum. If you write much more than 700 words, though, you should ask yourself:

- Have I understood the question properly?
- Is everything I am writing relevant to the question?
- Am I offering too many illustrations of my points?

Notes
The notes that follow refer to the numbered sections of the essay.
① This is a clear introduction which states the essay's main idea, that Bathsheba improves as time goes on.
② Despite the need not to retell the story, first impressions are a good way to start dealing with a character or setting, because they are the way in which the author introduces things to us.
③ The introduction ends with a hint as to how the essay is planned.
④ The topic of each paragraph (here, immaturity) is announced clearly in its first sentence.
⑤ The writer's idea (Bathsheba's vanity) is illustrated by reference to an incident briefly retold from the story.
⑥ An illustration is made by using a brief quotation from the text. The intelligent use of quotations makes it clear that you really know the text. Quotations that are too long make it look as though you do not understand what the most important words are. Keep most of your quotations to one or two sentences. (If you are revising for an examination that does not allow books in the room, you should learn twenty important quotations from each text. Only use them if they are relevant to your essay.)
⑦ The essay's change in direction (from bad traits to good ones) is clearly signposted by the first sentence of the new paragraph.
⑧ A point is illustrated briefly here without a quotation because no one quotation fully fitted the point being made.
⑨ The conclusion briefly reinforces the basic ideas behind the essay in the light of how it has turned out.

Worked Exercises

When you have finished your work, read it to yourself, checking for spelling and grammar, but also asking the following questions:
- Have I spelled the characters' names correctly?
- Is the plan behind the essay clear to the reader?
- Have I explained each point clearly enough?

If possible, now put your essay away for a couple of days, before rechecking it. You will find that you will see it more clearly coming to it afresh, and you may well be surprised at the number of improvements that you can make.

3. Essay Question Set in a Character's Voice

For this exercise we will return to *Hobson's Choice*, since the impression that you have gained of it from Question 1 (page 46 onwards) will help you appreciate the background to this essay.

> *What lessons might the other members of the Hobson family learn from Maggie's character and behaviour? Write, if you wish, in Maggie's voice.*

In this section we will see how you might set about answering the question "in Maggie's voice" – that is, as if Maggie herself were writing the answer. You may often wish to answer the questions in this way because you have been used to writing about literature through similar imaginative approaches – but do check with your teacher or with the examination paper that it is permitted to do so in each instance. At GCSE level, such questions demand the same factual accuracy of answer as questions that are not "voiced": you usually need to do them this way only if you find it easier to get your imagination going by doing so.

As it is set, this question poses a problem: you are allowed to adopt Maggie's voice, and therefore her viewpoint, but you are not told at what point in her life Maggie is supposed to be speaking – or indeed, whether she is supposed to be writing, speaking or just thinking. All these might make a difference to your answer: Maggie might, for instance, write in a different style from that in which she would speak; and she might have more insight into what was going on in her life at one time than another. The best questions will always tell you

when a character is speaking, thinking or writing;
whether they are speaking, thinking or writing;
why and *in what circumstances* they are doing it.

If the question that you are working on does not give these details, briefly think them out before you start writing, and work them if possible into the beginning of your essay. In the model answer, it is assumed that Maggie is much older, and that she is talking to her grandchildren: this puts her in a position where she has had a great deal of time to think about her life and to understand it, and it provides a good reason for imitating her voice as she speaks.

The point of the essay will be to display facts about the lives of Maggie and her family: quotations from and references to the play will be just as necessary as in any English Literature essay, but they will have to be worked in as Maggie's memories.

The further stages in preparing an essay like this are identical to those for preparing the essay in Question 2 (page 53 onwards): first, read through the text and make rough notes, and then reorganise the notes under headings. At this point you will probably realise that the essay is about themes or ideas arising from the text, and that these ideas arise from contrasts between Maggie's nature and the others' – that what she could teach them is about her nature, and that it could be summed up under headings such as:

> practicality
> imagination
> intelligence
> sincerity
> courage
> wit.

These can be used as a basis for deciding on the topics for the main paragraphs of the essay.

Before you read the following answer, a few facts about *Hobson's Choice* may help you. It is the story of Maggie Hobson, eldest daughter of Henry Horatio Hobson, a boot-maker in Salford in Victorian times: Hobson has lost control of his life – he is a weak man, a bully and an alcoholic. Maggie's sisters are shallow, silly creatures whose only idea in life is to get on by marrying someone well-off. Maggie, who seems to be on the shelf, since she is thirty and plain, is a great contrast: she is strong and intelligent. In the play she rescues her sisters from their father's bullying, puts their father in his place, and secures her future by marrying Willie Mossop, a craftsman boot-maker.

What lessons might the other members of the Hobson family learn from Maggie's character and behaviour? Write, if you wish, in Maggie's voice.

① So you want to know what your great-grandad and your great-aunts were like? It hurts me to say it, but my father was a shallow, selfish man, and my sisters were much the same. He was a vain, hypocritical, undisciplined bully, and Aunties Alice and

Worked Exercises

Vickey were little better – but there came a time when I showed them all!

② When we were young women, Father made us all work in the shop, and he was so mean that he wouldn't give us any money. Now money was always important to me – I always did the books in the shop, for instance – but I resolved that Alice and Vickey would get their fair share of it, and got Fred Beenstock to sue father for their dowries. Silly as they were, I couldn't be mean to them.

None of them were at all practical about life. Alice and Vickey got all sentimental about their young men, but couldn't lift a finger to get themselves married: it took me to achieve that. And when I left the shop, they could neither sell boots nor do the accounts. If only they could have taken a leaf out of my book! I knew our livelihood depended on our arithmetic and our selling; why, I even sold Albert Prosser boots when he came to court our Alice! They just didn't use their wits, whilst I was always full of schemes, whether to get them their dowries, or to put me and Willie in business, or to take over the Hobsons' shop. I used my imagination, and I could see the potential in Willie when he couldn't even read, whilst they could only see their way forward by marrying young men who were already well-off.

The worst thing about them all was that they were never really sincere. When Alice and Vickey heard that Father had a
③ breakdown, they came round, all full of sympathy, but then refused to come and live with him. "I live in the Crescent myself," said Alice; "My child comes first with me," said Vickey. At least I didn't pretend to be all soft with Father: I'd worked out how to look after him *and* do myself a good turn by making Willie a partner in the shop.

Father was just as hypocritical: he'd give us sermons on "good sense and sincerity", and then he'd go out and get drunk enough to fall down holes in the street. They could all have learnt from me. When I said, "Will Mossop, you're my man," I meant it, and I made sure that Will sincerely wanted to marry me before we went ahead with it. I kept quiet about my feelings, but they were strong and true. I still have the flower I pressed on my wedding day to remember it all by.

Though I say it myself, it took courage both to leave Father's shop for Willie, and then a year later to go back there again. Even

> though I have been forward as women go, it wasn't easy to have to confront Willie and tell him, "You're my man," for instance. Then coming back to my father when he'd had his breakdown was hard, too. I could only do it because by now Willie was able to take part of the strain, and negotiate with Father. If only I'd been able to train my sisters, too! But it was their inability to buckle down which left the way open for me to move in. They were left dependent on Fred Beenstock and Albert Prosser, whereas Willie and I worked as a team.
>
> My early life was quite hard, and if you ask me what kept me going, it was my sense of humour. I could tease my sisters about their gentlemen-friends, or Father about his lunch-time. I even had to tease Will into marrying me. None of my family had much sprightliness, though by the end of a year Will could hold his own with them as well as I could; but they'd never learn!
>
> ④ The truth is that to be sure of success in this life you have to be down-to-earth, practical, honest and courageous, and I've done my best to be all these things. My life would have been a lot easier if my father and sisters could have been like that, too.

Notes

① *The introductory section* makes the role and situation clear, as well as going over the basic ideas of the essay. The informal, chatty style is also established.
② Some *character points* are made by summarising part of the story . . .
③ . . . and some are made by quotation from the text, just as in the previous essay.
④ A *concluding section* has been worked in, so as to make sure the main points are expressed clearly.

- Study every essay title: make sure you fully understand it.
- Research relevant parts of the text from your book or from memory. If there is time, make notes.
- Plan the essay round a set of ideas, not just round the text's story-line.
- Think of your introduction and conclusion.
- Aim for 400-700 words unless told otherwise.
- Make each point by
  1. stating your idea;
  2. using a short summary of an incident or a quotation from the text;
  3. if necessary, explaining the quotation.
- Check your essay once or twice, if possible.

4 Getting the Most from Poetry

What Poetry Is

Oh no, not poetry!

Of all the types of writing studied for GCSE, poetry arouses the strongest reactions: it seems you must be either *for* it or *against* it. Those who dislike poetry say it is "too intellectual" or difficult; they probably feel that it is only read by "weird" people. Others, who never seem to be any weirder than the others, say that getting to grips with a poem is an experience they really enjoy. Arguably, though some poetry may at first be difficult and forbidding, poems are enjoyable, even fun, because they stimulate the imagination. After all, nearly every one of us responds to the lyrics of popular songs, which are basically a form of poetry composed for performance rather than the usual silent reading.

Form and Content

So what is poetry about? Why do people write it rather than prose? You will no doubt have got past the point of thinking that a poem is simply something that rhymes; and you will have noticed that though some poems do rhyme, many do not. What most poems have in common, however, is that they are written in separate lines whose length has been controlled by the writer. This is because writing in lines helps you to control the sound of what you are writing; and this is one aspect of the central fact about all poetry, that it is writing devised for the maximum possible effect. The effect may be instantly striking, like the opening of this poem:

> Why should I let the toad *work*
> Squat on my life?
> Can't I use my wit as a pitchfork
> And drive the brute off?
> (Philip Larkin)

or it may be subtle, puzzling, and intriguing, forcing you to think out what the poet really means, as in this example from the same poem:

> For something sufficiently toad-like
> Squats in me, too;
> Its hunkers are heavy as hard luck,
> And cold as snow.

It is this second type of poetry that some people give up on because it is difficult; others find it really satisfying to work things out for themselves. If you never try to work out the meaning of a difficult poem, you will never find out if it feels good to you.

Poetry, then, is a type of writing in which techniques are used intensively to produce effects and create meanings. So when you are assessed on poetry, you will often be asked to relate what you think a poem means and how it affects you, to the way it is written: this is called relating *content* (meaning and effects) to *form* (techniques). The important thing is to *start whenever possible from the content*, working out what the poem means and how it affects your feelings first, before going on to examine how the poem's form creates these meanings and feelings. This will prevent you from merely listing examples of techniques without showing their effects, and from inventing effects to go with techniques. Only work from techniques towards the poem's content if you are really stuck, or if a question forces you to do so.

- Poetry is writing devised for intensity of effect.
- Content is what a poem means and how it affects you.
- Form is how a poem is written, its technical features.
- Always try to see how a poem's form is brought about by its content, and not the other way round.

The Techniques of Poetry

Poetry and Prose

In Chapter 1, many technical features found in prose are mentioned: the relationships of words to meanings and feelings; the uses of similes, metaphors, personifications and symbols; sensuous language and the creation of words; sound-play and sentence-length – all these are found just as much in poetry as in prose. Some writers even believe that a richness of metaphors is the main formal feature of poetry, and you certainly will often find more comparisons in a poem than in a paragraph of prose. Poems do, however, use a number of techniques, some unique to poetry and others that are simply more common in poetry than in prose.

Verse

Earlier it was pointed out that poetry is written in separate lines of controlled length. The skill of writing effective lines is called *versification*, and it offers many techniques and effects.

Length of Lines. The length of the lines in which a poem is written affects the reader: it is as if we all have an idea of how long a line should be (probably derived from childhood knowledge of nursery rhymes and the length of phrase which is easiest to say out loud); we try to stretch out short lines to sound longer, and compress long ones to hurry them up. Thus, poems written in short lines read slowly:

> Into the dark tunnel
> from the white hills
> the train slows, almost
> stops.
>
> Across the aisle
> a man cups his eyes
> against the dark window.
> (Ian McMillan)

The slowness may be thoughtful, peaceful, sad or tense, according to the mood of the words.

Poems written in long lines tend to cause you to rush as you read them:

> Flow on, river! flow with the flood-tide, and ebb with the ebb-tide!
> Frolic on, crested and scallop-edged waves!
> Gorgeous clouds of the sunset! drench with your splendour me, or
>   the men and women generations after me!
> Cross from shore to shore, countless crowds of passengers!
> (Walt Whitman)

The effect of lines like these may be hurried or exciting, according to the mood of the words.

Often, a poet will vary the length of lines within a poem, as in this description of a mosquito:

> When did you start your tricks,
> Monsieur?
>
> What do you stand on such high legs for?
> Why this length of shredded shank,
> You exaltation?
>
> Is it that you shall lift your centre of gravity upwards
> And weigh no more than air as you alight upon me . . . ?
> (D. H. Lawrence)

The contrast between the differing lengths of line draws your attention to the different effects. The two short lines are given great emphasis – we tend to give a long pause at the end of them – and the two longest lines become hurried and almost tense. This shows how important the sound of poems is to their overall effect: if possible, you should always read a poem out loud (or listen to it being read) before you tackle it. In exam conditions you should try hard to imagine how the poem would sound if read by a good reader.

Pauses. When a poet is writing a poem in lines which are all the same length – perhaps in order to build up a steady rhythm – he or she can still hurry you up as you read, or slow you down and create emphasis, by controlling the number and position of pauses in the poem. This has a strong effect on the phrasing.

When we read a poem, we tend to expect a pause to occur at the end of each line:

> I wandered lonely as a cloud
>   That floats on high o'er vales and hills,
> When all at once I saw a crowd,
>   A host, of golden daffodils;
> Beside the lake, beneath the trees,
> Fluttering and dancing in the breeze.
> (William Wordsworth)

Note that in this quotation there is actually a slight pause at the end of the first line, even though there is no punctuation mark. Verse of this sort is what we grow to expect from the nursery rhymes and children's poetry of our early years. It has several good features: it makes a poem seem neat and orderly, and can give the impression that a poem is a piece of calm, considered thinking. On the other hand, if the rhythm is very strong or the rhyme is too insistent, it can sound childish; this effect is present on purpose in the next quotation, but it often occurs accidentally.

The Techniques of Poetry

> Little Lamb, who made thee?
> Dost thou know who made thee?
> Gave thee life, and bid thee feed,
> By the stream and o'er the mead . . .
> (William Blake)

Lines which end on a pause like this are called *end-stopped*. Most poets avoid the childish effect by varying the position of some of the pauses in their poems and by varying the number of pauses in each line, so that there is more than one pause per line or less than one. In the Wordsworth quotation just given, see how the poet has put in extra pauses after "a host" and "beside the lake". This prevents the poem from becoming too mechanical and makes the phrasing more varied and natural. In fact, Wordsworth is one of the most skilful poets at controlling rhythms and pauses.

As well as adding pauses, you can take them away:

> The blue jay scuffling in the bushes follows
> Some hidden purpose, and the gust of birds
> That spurts across the field, the wheeling swallows,
> Have nested in the trees and undergrowth.
> (Thom Gunn)

In these lines it is virtually impossible to pause after "follows" and "birds": the sense of the sentence requires that we read on to "purpose" and "field" respectively. This brings the poem alive by avoiding a repetitive pattern; lines like these are said to be *run on*, and the process of running-on is sometimes called *enjambement* (pronounced as if it were in French). Here, the running-on of the first line almost creates one very long line of poetry:

"The blue jay scuffling in the bushes follows Some hidden purpose." It is natural to read this in a tense, hurried way as it is quite a mouthful, so Gunn has got his poem off to a striking start. "And the gust of birds That spurts across the field" reads almost as if it were a single line of poetry, but it is still made memorable and a little tense by the lack of the expected pause after "birds". Finally, "the wheeling swallows", isolated between two pauses, reads much as if it were a short line on its own: it is natural to take such a short phrase slowly, and to emphasise it.

The three linked techniques of end-stopping, running-on and putting an extra pause in the middle of a line allow poets to phrase poems naturally, to create speed or slowness, haste and emphasis. Many good writers use them to great effect. Further, in poems with a tense mood, frustrating the reader's expectations for pauses can increase the tension noticeably.

Rhythm. In music you recognise immediately whether or not a tune has a strong rhythm, and whether the rhythm is fast or slow. Fast, strong rhythms have a lively effect, and are used for marching or dancing. Slow, gentle rhythms are suited to gentle subjects, such as romantic love songs. Poems have rhythms too, though they are often more subdued than those in music, and they are important in contributing to a poem's overall effect.

When we speak in English we tend to *stress* certain syllables more than others – that is to say, we say them a little louder. Read the following sentence aloud and see if you can spot the syllables that you stress:

Today is the sixteenth of February.

Put an accent like this ´ over the syllables you stressed.

Most people reading the sentence would put accents over the following syllables: *day, six, Feb*. Here is another prose sentence marked up with its stresses: the cupped accent ˘ is written over the relatively *un*stressed syllables:

Súndăy ĭs thĕ fírst dáy ŏf thĕ wéek.

In prose, the stresses come at random positions in the sentence, but one thing which poets may do is to write lines in which the stresses fall into an even pattern.

> Bŭt yés|tĕrdáy | thĕ wórd | ŏf Cáe|săr míght
>
> Hăve stóod | ăgáinst | thĕ wórld: | nŏw líes | hĕ thére
>
> (Shakespeare)

> Thĕ fáir | brĕeze bléw, | thĕ whíte | fŏam fléw,
>
> Thĕ fúr|rŏw fól|lŏwed frée.
>
> (Coleridge)

These two samples show the basic two-beat rhythm of English poetry: the first, from Shakespeare, has five beats to the line, and is typical of the lines used when plays are written in verse; the second has four beats to one line and three beats to the next, alternately, and is typical of a great deal of narrative poetry. Lines of these lengths and with these rhythms have a largely neutral effect: they are what we tend to expect when we read a poem. Variations from these patterns are often worth commenting on, however.

The Techniques of Poetry

The basic repeated unit in the lines we have looked at has been ˘ ´ (ti-tum); we call this a *foot*. There are many other types of feet available to a poet to use, including the following.

    ´ ˘ (tum-ti)   ˘ ˘ ´ (ti-ti-tum)   ´ ´ (tum-tum)
    ˘ ˘ (ti-ti)   ´ ˘ ˘ (tum-ti-ti)

One thing that a poet can do is to put one or more of these less common feet into a basically regular line: this will have the effect of making it sound more natural, and may have deeper effects. In a famous passage Coleridge swaps round some of the stresses and shortens the lines:

> Wátĕr, | wátĕr, | évĕrў | whére,
>
> Nŏr ănlў dróp | tŏ drínk.
>   (Coleridge)

These lines seem heavier, sadder and more emphatic because of this. The more stressed syllables you can get in a line, the heavier it becomes:

> Bréak, bréak, bréak,
>
> Oň thў cóld | grĕy stónes, | Ŏ Séa!
>   (Tennyson)

The unconventional first line here underlines the poet's misery as well as imitating the beat of the waves. In the following line, Browning uses feet with two light beats to make the line rush along.

> Ĭ gál | lŏped, Dĭrck gál | lŏped, wĕ gál | lŏped ăll thrée.

Once again there is imitation here – the rhythm is like the beat of horses' hooves – but imitation is not necessary for this sort of effect. Introducing light beats into a line will always make it skip along in a way suitable for happy and active subjects.

For GCSE, you do not necessarily need to be able to mark the stresses and foot-divisions on a line, but it does help if you can spot
1. how many beats there are to a line;
2. whether all, or most, lines are the same;
3. whether the rhythm is regular or varied;
4. if there are extra light or heavy syllables.

Two words of warning are needed:
1. Rhythm is worth commenting on only if it has an effect on the mood of the poem.

2. Many poets – especially modern ones – do not write in feet, but use much looser forms of rhythm. Do not invent feet where there are none!
- Line length affects speed, mood and emphasis.
- Rhythm affects speed, weight, mood and emphasis.
- Lines following a regular pattern can seem dull and mechanical.
- Slight variations of length and rhythm can make verse sound more natural.

Sound-play

The sounds made by the different letters in words are a rich source of effects in poems. Rhyme is the most obvious technique using this aspect of sound, but it is not necessarily the most important one.

Rhyme. We normally expect English poetry to rhyme, but many types of poem are in unrhymed verse. Originally, before everyone could read, one reason for using rhyme was to make verse easy to memorise, but it has other effects, too. Rhymes make line endings more obvious, and make it possible to write very neat poems where each thought fits into two-lined rhymes:

> On her white breast a sparkling cross she wore,
> Which Jews might kiss, and infidels adore.
> (Alexander Pope)

In these lines Pope neatly expresses the point that the girl's attractions might make men go against their religions. Pairs of lines like these, which stand next to each other and rhyme, are known as *couplets*. Poems can be written in couplets, but they tend to sound artificial and monotonous unless rhythms and pauses are used skilfully. Writers of long poems and plays tend to prefer *blank verse*, with no rhymes, as sounding more natural. Most rhyming poems have alternate lines which rhyme, or an even more complicated *rhyme scheme* like this:

> Fair daffodils, we weep to see
> You haste away so soon:
> As yet the early-rising sun
> Has not attain'd his noon.
> Stay, stay,
> Until the hasting day
> Has run
> But to the evensong;
> And, having pray'd together, we
> Will go with you along.
> (Robert Herrick)

The Techniques of Poetry

In poems like this, the effect of rhyme alone is hardly noticeable: it needs to be considered in conjunction with the following sound-effects.

Assonance and Alliteration. These techniques involve the repetition of the same or similar sounds. *Assonance* is the repetition of vowels (the sounds made by A,E,I,O,U, Y when it sounds like I, and combinations of these letters), whilst *alliteration* is the repetition of consonants (the sounds made by all the other letters). Pairs of alliterated words can often catch your attention – it is a good way of emphasising an idea:

> We are the music-makers,
> We are the dreamers of dreams.
> (O'Shaughnessy)

Both "music-makers" and "dreamers of dreams" stand out because of the repeated sounds.

If a poem contains a great deal of assonance and alliteration, coupled with rhymes, it will sound sweet and musical. Listen to the repeated Ls, Ss and Ts, together with the rhymes, in this verse:

> Look, stranger, on this island now
> The leaping light for your delight discovers,
> Stand stable here
> And silent be,
> That through the channels of the ear
> May wander like a river
> The swaying sound of the sea.
> (W. H. Auden)

This sweetness is appropriate here because it enhances the beauty of the scene.

We can identify even more effects of sound-play. Vowels can be classified as short and long, consonants as hard and soft. Poems soaked in short and hard sounds seem brittle and energetic: read aloud the quotation from Browning on page 70 and listen to its Gs, As, Ps, and Ds. Anger can often be expressed this way. On the other hand, a poem full of long and soft sounds can sound sweet, sad or sleepy: read again the quotation from Herrick and pay attention to its EEs, As, Ss and Ns. When you say them, long and soft sounds can be prolonged for ever – or at least until you run out of breath – whilst short and hard ones cannot be lengthened. Hard consonants will not lengthen at all, and short vowels change their characters entirely and become new, long sounds. Try lengthening the consonants in *mean* and *bad*, and the vowels in *get* and *cheese* in order to hear this contrast.

VOWELS	CONSONANTS
SHORT	HARD
a (as in *hat*)	b
e (as in *bet*)	c (as in *cap*)
i (as in *hit*)	d
o (as in *hot*)	g (as in *get*)
u (as in *hut*)	k
y (as in *pity*)	p
	q
	t
LONG	SOFT
a (as in *hate*)	c (as in *juice*)
e (as in *scene*)	f
i (as in *bite*)	g (as in *judge*)
o (as in *hope*)	h
u (as in *flute*)	j ch
y (as in *rhyme*)	l sh
	m
(There are also long vowel sounds made by pairs of letters, such as: ai, ea, ei, ie, oe, oi, ou, oy, etc.)	n
	r
	s
	v
	w
	x
	z

Onomatopoeia. This is a rather specialised sound-effect. A few words actually sound like the thing they represent: examples are *bang*, *bark*, *howl* and *clap*. The use of words like this is known as *onomatopoeia*, and it can have two levels of effect: at the very least it will make a poem vivid by catching the reader's attention; but when well done, it can give the poem the same mood that listening to the original sound would produce. Keats, in the following line, describes the sadness with which some of the sounds of autumn affect him, reminding him that summer is over:

"Then in a wailful choir the small gnats mourn."

We can almost hear the insects buzzing, and feel the poet's sadness, too.

- Rhyme, assonance and alliteration work together to produce: musicality, sweetness, harshness, or to catch the attention.
- Onomatopoeia helps you recall sounds and their associations.

A Warning

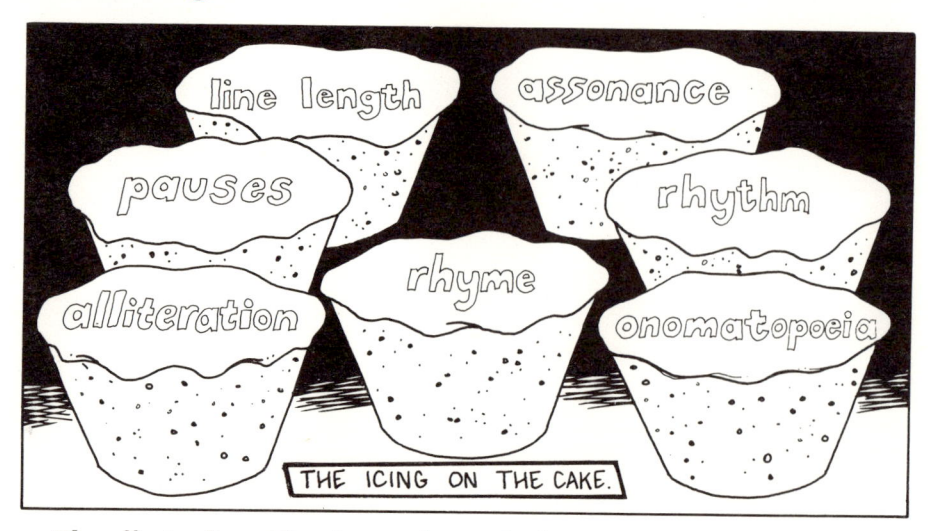

[Illustration of cupcakes labelled with: line length, assonance, pauses, rhythm, alliteration, rhyme, onomatopoeia. Caption: THE ICING ON THE CAKE.]

The effects of versification and sound-play are complex and subtle. It has therefore taken quite a lot of space to explain them. But do not run away with the idea that they are the most important technical aspects of poetry. The meaning of words, the use of words to convey attitudes and moods, and the use of imagery (as described in Chapter 1) are the basis of most of the effects of poetry just as they are of prose. Versification and sound-play are only the icing on the cake, but if you can make sensible comments about the effects they have, you will gain credit for showing that you are sensitive to them.

Tackling a Poem

Often you will have a teacher's help in first coming to understand a poem, either as he or she leads the discussion, or through a set of questions. You do need to be able to understand poems unaided, however, as you may be asked to prepare one for homework, and even when you are answering questions, your answers will be better if they stem from a full understanding of the poem.

This section will show you how to tackle a famous poem when reading it for the first time. First, check what your basic ideas about it are, and how you have reacted to it emotionally; then go through it checking that you understand its meaning in detail, both at the denotative and the connotative levels. In this reading, you should attempt to understand all the imagery involved. Next, look for other features that may have affected your reactions, such as versification and sound-play. Finally, try to sum up what the poem means to you.

Normally, of course, this work would be done in your head, or by means of rough notes.

The poem has no title, and is by the nineteenth-century poet Tennyson.

> Now sleeps the crimson petal, now the white;
> Nor waves the cypress in the palace walk;
> Nor winks the gold fin in the porphyry[1] font:
> The fire-fly wakens: waken thou with me.
>
> Now droops the milkwhite peacock like a ghost,
> And like a ghost she glimmers on to me.
>
> Now lies the earth all Danaë[2] to the stars,
> And all thy heart lies open unto me.
>
> Now slides the silent meteor on, and leaves
> A shining furrow, as thy thoughts in me.
>
> Now folds the lily all her sweetness up,
> And slips into the bosom of the lake:
> So fold thyself, my dearest, thou, and slip
> Into my bosom and be lost in me.
>
> [1] *porphyry*: an ornamental stone used in ancient Egypt, reddish-purple in colour.
> [2] *Danaë*: a princess loved by Zeus in Greek mythology. He visited her in prison, as a shower of gold.

First Impressions

The poem seems to be about a meeting, at night, between two lovers. The effect is very emotional, and there is a sense of its being a rich, intense experience. The poem seems rich descriptively, too: it is full of pictures.

Comments. Note how these instant reactions range widely over the poem's meaning, feelings, and other contents. You might equally have put something in about its technique if it had struck you strongly at this stage. There is no need to add all these impressions together or come to an overall understanding of the poem yet: concentrate on opening up the poem's possibilities.

Detailed Reactions

It is now time to go through the poem detail by detail, trying to add up the ways it conveys both meanings and feelings to you. The first section is a description of night-time in which the stillness of nature is stressed.

Words are used in unusual ways to suggest peacefulness; for instance, the petals are said to "sleep", which is a metaphor, as only animals and humans sleep. Perhaps it suggests the way in which some flowers close up at night, as if closing their eyes to the outside world. The use of "nor" in "nor waves . . . nor winks" without "neither" is unusual and centres our attention on what is *not* happening, such as the normal movement of foliage in the breeze and the flashing of light on the fishes' fins. The fishes' movement is hidden in the darkness. This is contrasted with the brightness and liveliness of the night-time creature, the fire-fly, and the intensity of its night-time existence symbolises that of the lovers.

This section isn't only about the quietness of night and the intensity of the lovers' experience, however: it also suggests a sense of richness in what is going on. Literal riches are implied in the setting, a palace, with a fountain in its garden. There is a richness of sensuous detail, too, in the colours, crimson, white and gold. The word "font" suggests that the fountain is almost holy. Thus, the intensity of the love is expressed by contrast both to stillness and peace and to richness and luxury.

Each of the remaining sections is also composed of a picture from the setting of the lovers' meeting and part of that meeting itself. In these sections, however, the parts do not contrast; they parallel each other, intensifying each other by their emotional similarity. We could say that the elements from the setting are used to symbolise aspects of the meeting.

First the lover's approach is paired with the appearance of a white peacock. Peacocks are beautiful and exotic birds, and white ones are rare; these qualities are passed on to the lover. Whiteness also suggests gentleness and purity. Both bird and lover are compared to ghosts, partly because they are indistinct in the dark, and therefore mysterious, and partly, perhaps, to suggest the spirituality of the lovers' feelings.

The earth's openness to the glittering night sky is compared first to Danaë and then to openness of the lover's heart, or inner being. Who was Danaë? Looking her up in the footnote, we find that she was a mythical ancient Greek princess, who was visited by her lover Zeus in the form of a shower of gold. Again, this is an image of richness which has the effect of suggesting the lover's total openness, giving it both a mystical and a sexual quality. As in all the verses, the quality of love is symbolised by light (fire-fly, "milkwhite peacock", meteor and lily) in the encircling darkness. It is as if love lights up the speaker's life.

A shooting-star crosses the sky, appearing momentarily to leave a bright trace on the sky; thoughts about his lover (or remembering his lover's thoughts, or both) leave such traces on the speaker's soul. Yet it is all "silent", peaceful, not violent or fiery.

The image of flowers folding up for the night is returned to: water-lilies apparently submerge when they do this. It is described in personification: the flower "slips into the bosom" of the lake, a picture of an intimate embrace. This leads the poet naturally to desire a similar embrace, where the girl can "be lost in me" – can abandon her thoughts and cares, lose track of the real world in his arms.

Comment. At this stage you have worked through the poem trying to note as much as you can about its meaning and the feelings it expresses, and to relate these to matters of technique.

Sounds and Rhythms

Reading the poem, you are very conscious that it *sounds* beautiful, that it has a rich, musical quality which strengthens the richness and beauty of its description. Yet its rhythm is a neutral, regular five beats to the line. Rhyme is hardly used – just in the way each verse ends in "me", which emphasises that the poem is about the relationship, not just about the girl.

There is a subtle pattern of assonance and alliteration based on long vowels and soft consonants, such as the repeated *or* and *y* vowels, and the *n, m, s, w* and *f* consonants in the first verse.

> Now sleeps the crimson petal, now the white;
> Nor waves the cypress in the palace walk;
> Nor winks the gold fin in the porphyry font:
> The fire-fly wakens: waken thou with me.

This seems to be typical of the poem's music.

Comment. Here you noticed sound-qualities after looking at the poem's meanings and feelings. This is possible because the sound-qualities are constant throughout the poem. In other poems the sound quality changes from line to line, expressing first one feeling then another; in a poem of this sort it is probably best to tackle the sound at the same time as the meanings. You will always need to adapt the way in which you tackle each individual poem to the nature of the poem itself.

Final Check

Quickly reread the poem to see if there is anything that you have missed. Note, for instance, that the last verse continues the description of a physically rich and luxurious setting: the lily-studded lake is obviously part of the palace-complex mentioned at the beginning. And returning to the beginning, notice that the tree is a cypress, a variety not often found in Britain. Are we to imagine an exotic Mediterranean setting for the poem, perhaps Danaë's Greece?

Comment. Whenever you reread a poem, you will almost always find something new to say.

Summing Up

This poem expresses the feelings of a man as he meets his lover by night. It expresses the richness of experience by comparing it to the richness of the setting, a luxurious palace in a southern country. The heart of the experience is both spiritual or emotional, and physical. The spiritual dimension is emphasised by the symbols and metaphors of the ghost, Danaë, the stars, and whiteness and light. The poem has a strong physical presence, however: it is full of sensuous description, and the reference to Danaë also introduces a note of sexuality, which is picked up by the image of the closing lines. The intensity of the experience is ecstatic, amounting to losing one's self-consciousness. The richness of the poem's subject is matched by a rich, musical use of sound.

Comment. If you were writing an essay or talking to a group about the poem, you would need these conclusions *first*, before writing your introduction. Only by starting with a clear view of the whole of a poem can you hope to write an orderly and complete essay or script.

- Read a poem twice before starting to work on its detail.
- Try to start with your general impressions of its meanings and effect, rather than with a list of technical features you have found.
- Then try to relate meaning and effect (*content*) to techniques (*form*).
- Adapt your approach to the poem.
- Try to reach some conclusions which state
  1. the poem's theme,
  2. how it affects your feelings,
  3. what range of techniques is used.

5 Writing About Poetry

How to Write About a Poem

Types of Question

An analysis of a single poem, such as the one in the previous chapter, will form the foundation for the answers to two types of exercise. *Unseen Appreciation* exercises on poetry are similar to those on prose: a poem is printed, along with three or four short questions. In an examination, this poem will not come from a set book; but in coursework, it may well be from a set book, so long as the poem has not previously been discussed in class. *Essay Questions* on a single poem usually ask you about one specific aspect of the poem, though you may be sure that you will need to understand the poem fully in order to do the question well. In examination conditions you will usually either find the poem printed for you on the paper, or be able to take your poetry text into the exam room with you.

1. Unseen Appreciation

The following is a typical unseen appreciation exercise. You may like to attempt the questions (on paper or in your head) before you read the answers to them.

Read the following poem carefully, and answer the questions that follow.

> Now sleeps the crimson petal, now the white;
> Nor waves the cypress in the palace walk;
> Nor winks the gold fin in the porphyry[1] font:
> The fire-fly wakens: waken thou with me.
>
> Now droops the milkwhite peacock like a ghost,
> And like a ghost she glimmers on to me.
>
> Now lies the earth all Danaë[2] to the stars,
> And all thy heart lies open unto me.
>
> Now slides the silent meteor on, and leaves
> A shining furrow, as thy thoughts in me.
>
> Now folds the lily all her sweetness up,
> And slips into the bosom of the lake:
> So fold thyself, my dearest, thou, and slip
> Into my bosom and be lost in me.

[1] *porphyry*: an ornamental stone used in ancient Egypt, reddish-purple in colour.
[2] *Danaë*: a princess loved by Zeus in Greek mythology. He visited her in prison, as a shower of gold.

1. Choose two short descriptions or phrases from the poem, and say why you find them effective.
2. Choose two comparisons from the poem and explain their effect on the reader.
3. How does the poet use contrast in the first section of the poem?

Answer 1
"Nor winks the gold fin." In this description, the word "gold" not only tells us the colour of the fish, it also associates it with riches. The shininess of gold is picked up in the word "winks" which catches the way in which fish cast sudden bright reflections, as an eye does.

"The milkwhite peacock." This is an unexpected phrase, as peacocks are usually blue and green. It captures the strangeness of the moment, and implies that the bird is a gentle sight, as milk is not a bright white and is associated with purity and childhood.

Answer 2
"Like a ghost she glimmers on to me." This comparison shows that the girl is indistinct to see, yet pale, in the darkness of the night. It hints that the writer finds it almost hard to believe in her presence.

"And slips into the bosom of the lake." This phrase personifies the lily; it shows that the poet is already thinking about the tender embrace of the last line, and imagining its all-enveloping quality: the lily is lost in the lake just as the lover is lost in his embrace.

Answer 3
The first three lines of the poem stress sleepiness, darkness and the lack of activity. The closed petals are imagined as sleeping, and everything is seen as still: this is stressed by the unusual use of "nor" before the action-verbs "waves" and "winks". In contrast, the fire-fly "wakens" and gives off light, which gives a sense of the wakefulness that the lovers feel.

Comment. Notice the way in which the first two questions force you to pick on words or phrases and comment on them. Of course, you could have chosen other examples than the ones above. The more you can say about each phrase (barring information irrelevant to the question) the better. Even the third question demands that you talk about the effect of individual words. It is not, of course, ever enough simply to say that words or phrases are "effective": you always need to say in what way they affect you – by sensuous description, by arousing feelings, and so on.

2. Essays on a Single Poem

Exercises of this type are generally very open, almost inviting you to write everything you know about the poem. They do, however, give you a direction to work in, and require a planned approach: you will see how important it is to have worked your way through the poem first. Occasionally, this sort of question will require some knowledge of the set book outside the poem in question: keep your eyes peeled for such a trap.

Here are some questions which might be set on the Tennyson poem. Each is designed to be answered in 400-600 words.

Question 1. What appeals to you about this poem? Write about what you find interesting in it, referring to the effects created by individual words and phrases.

> *Question 2.* How does Tennyson create vivid descriptive effects and a strong sense of feeling in his poem?
>
> *Question 3.* If you were reading this poem for the first time, how would you recognise that it is by Tennyson?

Comment. It should be plain that Questions 1 and 2 can be answered simply by organising and selecting materials from the notes made after your initial reading of the poem. Question 1 does not need to be a total analysis of the poem; you do not need to have mastered every detail to answer it. Your answer will be confused, however, if you have not reached clear conclusions about the poem (see page 78) before you start.

For Question 2 you need to select *only* comments relevant to description and mood, and you need some ideas to introduce the essay with – which say briefly what Tennyson's techniques are – before exploring them in detail. Once more, a set of preliminary conclusions will help you with this.

Question 3, of course, demands that you know more about Tennyson. In fact, sensuous description, strong emotion and romantic settings are all typical of his work; it would be unwise to attempt to answer the question without this further knowledge, however.

3. Comparison Questions

Frequently you will come across types of question which invite you to write about more than one poem. There are three basic types.

1. *Questions about a technique* – e.g. Show how the writers appeal to the reader's senses in at least two poems from the collection.

2. *Questions about an effect* – e.g. Choose three poems that affect your feelings strongly and show how each author achieves this effect.

3. *Questions about a theme* – e.g. Choose two or three poems on love or affection, and write about how the poet has made them convincing in each case.

Each of these questions invites you to home in on one aspect of two or three poems that you know. The problem for you in examinations is knowing which aspect you will have to write about. It is obvious that question-spotting would be extremely hazardous, especially when it comes to examination revision.

The message is clear: whether you are writing about a technique or an effect or a theme, there really is no substitute for having a complete overall picture of each poem you have studied, and then practising essay-plans that select ideas from the overviews.

Worked Exercise

Let us look at the second of the questions printed opposite, and see how you might tackle it with regard to *one* of the three poems. Suppose you found the following poem in the collection that you were using:

> ### Not Waving But Drowning
>
> Nobody heard him, the dead man,
> But still he lay moaning;
> I was much further out than you thought
> And not waving but drowning.
>
> Poor chap, he always loved larking
> And now he's dead
> It must have been too cold for him his heart gave way,
> They said.
>
> Oh, no no no, it was too cold always
> (Still the dead one lay moaning)
> I was much too far out all my life
> And not waving but drowning.
>
> (Stevie Smith)

Again, let's work from first impressions and detailed reactions towards an answer, which in this case will be a planned-out, orderly section of an essay.

First Impressions

The poem hinges round a metaphor, which says that the life of the dead man was like a process of drowning in deep cold water. This is in itself frightening. The coldness in question probably means emotional coldness, the callousness or stand-offishness of people that the man knew.

Detailed Reactions

The first line creates an eerie atmosphere, for how can one hear a dead man, unless he is a ghost? This ghostliness is picked up in line 2, with the word "moaning". His words "I was much further out than you thought" suggest that he was out of his depth in some emotional way, but give it a physical immediacy, and the idea that his frantic gestures (his attempts to communicate) were mistaken for happy ones shows how people turn a blind eye to life's unhappy side. This is borne out when the people see him as having been "larking" (having fun), instead of acting

Worked Exercise

being happy to try and make friends. The people again miss the point when they think it was the cold water which killed him: it was their coldness which drove him to suicide.

The misery of the poem is expressed by the sounds it makes. The light, unstressed endings of some of the lines give it a feeling of ironic gaiety, which the long heavy vowels of the "no no no" contradict.

Sample Answer

To arrive at an orderly answer, pick out the following themes from the notes:
1. the basic metaphor;
2. feelings from the diction;
3. feelings from the sound-play.

> "Not Waving But Drowning" is a bitter, ironic poem. It works on our emotions on at least three different levels: the base metaphor, the connotations of the language and the sound of the poem.
>
> The poem's feelings come in the first instance from the metaphor which is at its basis, of a man's despair and suicide being like his drowning in cold water. People's coldness is just as lethal, it is implied, and it is just as easy to get out of your depth in life as it is in the sea. These thoughts are bitter and pessimistic, and made more vivid by the comparison with physical drowning.
>
> The irony of the poem is that the victim's pretence of happiness has been mistaken for the real thing, and so we get pairs of words whose connotations contrast:
>
> "Not *waving* but *drowning*"
> ". . . he always loved *larking*
> And now he's *dead*"
>
> The saddest phrase, which again combines physical and emotional connotations, is "his heart gave way": physically he died from heart failure, but emotionally it was from heartbreak.
>
> The poem's sound emphasises its bitterness. The light line endings ("móanĭng", "drównĭng", "lárkĭng", and so on) give it a false lightness of touch, which makes it bitter. The heavy sounds of "Oh, no no no" put an end to this, however, and allow us to feel grief for the suicide.

- Check whether questions can be done unseen or need background knowledge.
- Always anchor your answers on references to individual words and phrases.
- Avoid answering questions on set-book poems which you do not already understand fully.

6 Wider Reading

Personal Responses

One of the characteristics of GCSE English Literature is the insistence in every syllabus that the work submitted by candidates should show their *personal response* to literature. This means that it is no longer any good simply to learn your teacher's opinions about books parrot-fashion, or to swallow ideas whole from textbooks. You will need to show in all your work that you understand what you are saying, and can apply the techniques of reading both to texts you have studied and to extracts you are seeing for the first time.

The insistence on personal responses is also partly responsible for another new feature of GCSE English Literature syllabuses: it is known as the *Open Study* or *Wider Reading*. The detailed regulations for this vary from syllabus to syllabus, but in all of them you have to submit at least one piece of coursework that shows you have read outside the set books chosen by the examining group or by your teacher. Sometimes the choice of books is left entirely up to you and your teacher; in other cases, a list of suitable books for wider reading is supplied.

Basically, then, a wider reading essay deals with more than one book. Indeed, you may find that the regulations for your syllabus specify that your work covers *more than one form* – that is, your essay may have to cover prose plus drama, drama plus poetry or prose plus poetry (or all three). You will be dealing with two or three texts in each essay, and the basic skill in doing this successfully is knowing how to choose books that are linked by a single topic.

Choosing Texts and Topics

Texts by the Same Author

One possible link is that between books by the same author. For instance, you could read a selection of books by Laurie Lee: *Cider with Rosie*, which you may already have come across, plus *As I Walked Out One Midsummer Morning* and a selection of his poems. You could then try to find out what they have in common – what shows them to be products of the same mind. You might decide that qualities such as rich descriptive style, use of imagery and careful, rhythmic phrasing are always present in Lee's style, or you might concentrate on his fascination with places, people and anecdotes. Either of these possibilities could be turned into a plan for an essay: your main difficulty might be in keeping the piece short enough, as you will have to choose several incidents or quotations from each text.

Studying a Genre

Another way of choosing texts to write about is to choose two or three from the same *genre*. A genre is a recognised type of book, such as detective fiction, war fiction, romantic fiction or science fiction. (You could equally choose murder mystery plays or certain types of comedy.) The best way of handling a genre study is to try and see similarities between books, and to work out to what extent two authors (or two works by the same author) are following the same rules. If we took Hardy's *Far from the Madding Crowd* and Jane Austen's *Pride and Prejudice* and studied them as romantic fiction, we could uncover some interesting rules. Both heroines are pretty, intelligent and lively; but on the bad side, they are both headstrong and vain. Both want to fall in love with a handsome, dashing man, and both regret doing so. In fact, they both end up with a suitor who is not obviously attractive, whom they have previously rejected. These similarities are in fact very interesting: they begin to suggest to us that there were set ways of thinking about romance in the last century. On the other hand, you could also study the differences between the texts – one has a strong, plain hero and the other a weak but attractive one – and demonstrate each author's unique point of view.

Studying a Theme

An obvious way of choosing two linked pieces of work is to find books that share a similar theme, or set of ideas. This is particularly useful if you have to cover more than one type of writing in an essay. For instance, if you wanted to choose parents and teachers as a theme, you might pick on the play *A Taste of Honey* by Shelagh Delaney and the novel *Billy Liar* by Keith Waterhouse, both written in the early 1960s. You would be able to find many similarities in the sorts of problem causing friction between the generations in these two books: parents who are set in their ways, shut into their own minds, unaware of their children's feelings and needs, play a big part in both texts. The children are, in their turn, rebellious, sarcastic, satirical and emotionally immature. The hopelessness of this situation is stressed in both texts by unhappy endings in which the characters fail to escape from their destructive ways of life. You might leave your essay at that, concluding that it is interesting that two writers at about the same time were thinking so similarly; or you might go on to study more texts on the same theme from the same period – for instance, some of Alan Sillitoe's short stories – and conclude that this type of thinking must have been common at the time.

Studying a Period

The type of essay described above is an example of studying texts linked by a period, and this can be a good basis for comparisons. There should preferably be at least one other common factor between the texts: this might be genre, theme or characterisation.

You should also check your choice of books carefully with your teacher, because you will need to know whether, and in what ways, the texts are typical of their period. The poems of both Tennyson and Browning were written in the Victorian age, for example; but Tennyson's musical-sounding verse is much more typical of the period than Browning's tendency to imitate the sounds of lively and natural speaking voices.

Studying Heroes and Heroines

By comparing heroes of similar types of story written at different times, you can begin to see what factors were considered worthwhile in men; in the examples of *Far from the Madding Crowd* and *Pride and Prejudice* given above, you can see a type of reliable nineteenth-century hero; on the other hand, if you read Ernest Hemingway's *A Farewell to Arms* and F. Scott Fitzgerald's *The Great Gatsby*, you will see two very different definitions of heroism from the 1920s.

Heroines can be even more interesting. Feminists today insist that women should be strong, assertive, level-headed and independent. It is a useful exercise to take heroines from the past and see to what extent they are stereotyped as foolish, emotional, weak and dependent on men. The heroines of some of Shakespeare's comedies, such as Rosalind in *As You Like It* and Viola in *The Merchant of Venice*, are particularly interesting in this respect, as they spend much of the play disguised successfully as men! Beware, however: *only tackle Shakespeare on your own if you are really sure you can do it.*

If you do so, make sure that you see a performance or video of each play: this will make the plot and characters much clearer.

Other Comparisons

Many other bases for comparisons between sets of texts can be found. Differences between the same story told as a novel and a play can be interesting, as can studies of the treatment of a historical period or place in the work of different authors. You will always be on the lookout for what the different texts have in common as well as what makes them unique.

- Choose texts in pairs or sets linked by common factors such as themes, character-types, genres and periods.

Getting the Best out of Your Teacher

Getting the Best out of Your Teacher

Your wider reading work is meant to be your own personal project, but do take note of advice given to you by your teacher. You may be irritated if your teacher tells you that a book you want to write about is "unsuitable". By all means try to get him or her to explain just why this is so, but do respect your teacher's judgement. The reasons may not simply be that one book is a classic whilst another is not: over the years, a good teacher will have developed an instinct for which authors and types of book will provide you with enough to write about, and which ones will not.

Choose at least one book yourself for each essay you have to write; but then do be willing to go to your teacher for help in choosing the ones to put with it. He or she should be able to suggest to you books that can be compared to your choice in more than one way, thus opening up the possibility of writing more than one piece on the same set of books.

Do not hide your notes and plans from your teacher. Even if your Further Reading work is meant to be done at home, bring your essay plans into class and discuss them with your teacher: ambush the poor soul between lessons if necessary, but do it!

Talking things over is a legitimate part of doing work on your own. Finally remember that, as with all your other English coursework, your teacher is allowed to read a rough draft of your essay and make comments. These do not amount to marking your draft in detail, but can take the form of useful general ideas – perhaps about points you have made badly, or missed out, or even over-emphasised. Such criticisms can be useful when polishing up the final version of your essay, and can make you feel more confident about your final grades.

Remember, though, that in all your English Literature work, however it is assessed, it is *your* views and *your* knowledge that will gain you a good grade. Facts parroted from lessons and books may get you so far, but will not get you a boosted grade. Use the ideas and skills mentioned in this book to make yourself able to understand and appreciate what you read for yourself.

- Accept your teacher's advice on what texts to use for Further Reading.
- Consult with your teacher at every stage of your study.
- Only write what you believe and understand.

Wider Reading Essay

In the following pages, this type of essay is approached by referring to three books already dealt with in previous chapters: you will certainly have picked up a little about each book, and this will make it easier to understand what follows. In real life, of course, you would not normally be dealing with the same books in this part of your syllabus as in other parts: certainly the ones you would use would not normally be on your set-book list. Let's pretend that you have been reading *Jane Eyre*, *Far from the Madding Crowd* and *Hobson's Choice*, and that your teacher has dreamed up the following question for you:

> *Compare the heroines in the three texts that you have read. Which do you consider to be the most independent, and which do you prefer?*

The stages to go through for this essay are the same as those for a single text: study the title, do your research, plan the essay, then write it and check it.

1. *The title.* This asks you to write about each of the three heroines, and to concentrate on two aspects: (a) their independence, and (b) how much you like them. The first of these is a single character-trait, which needs to be studied in detail, but the second depends on their characters as a whole, which you will have to sketch in also.

2. *Research.* Your note-making should therefore be limited to the two aspects mentioned, i.e. the heroines' independence and your liking for them. You will not need too many notes on each text, as each should feature only as one third of the essay. If you are confident enough, and

know your text well, you will be able to get away with a very few notes on each book; if you are unsure, it is clearly best to have more than you will need.

3. *Planning.* This is a comparison essay in which you will be looking for similarities and contrasts between the three heroines. Before you start, therefore, make up some headings from your rough notes, and try to organise them into a three-column format like this.

Jane Eyre	Bathsheba E.	Maggie Hobson
Independence	Early independence – mistakes – later dependence on Oak	Independence
Intelligence Practicality despite passion	Intelligence Some practicality but swayed by emotion	Intelligence Practicality
Sense of humour	Teasing } Vanity }	Sense of humour
Imagination		Imagination
Moral principles despite passion	Learns some principles	Economic principles

There are clearly two different ways of organising your plan into an essay: you can either work down the columns or along the lines. The first approach would give you an essay in three main sections, one each on Jane, Bathsheba and Maggie. The second would give six sections, on independence, intelligence, practicality, humour and vanity, imagination, and principles. Each of these sections would refer to Jane, Bathsheba and Maggie in turn. Although the second way appears to give you the greatest scope for making comparisons, the first is probably preferable, as it is easier to organise, and in this case it will leave a clearer picture of the three women. Before putting pen to paper, try to sum up the differences between the women briefly in note form, so that you can write an introduction to give the reader a clear idea of what would follow.

Wider Reading Essay

Jane Eyre	Bathsheba E.	Maggie Hobson
Best balanced character	Likeable but flawed character	Strong, successful, but could be too hard.

A possible essay would look like this:

Compare the heroines in the three texts that you have read. Which do you consider to be the most independent, and which do you prefer?

①   In this essay I am going to write about Jane Eyre, Bathsheba Everdene from *Far from the Madding Crowd*, and Maggie
② Hobson from *Hobson's Choice*. All three try to be strong, independent women, but Bathsheba's faulty judgement leads her to become dependent on Gabriel Oak. Maggie Hobson is independent enough to lead her husband, Willie, but I find her lacking in some kinds of warmth. Overall, I prefer Jane Eyre, who combines independence and determination with a warm, passionate nature.

③   At the beginning of *Far from the Madding Crowd* we see Bathsheba's weaknesses clearly. Her long look at herself in the
④ mirror is well described by Gabriel as "vanity", and her impulsiveness and lack of consideration come out when she chases after him only to refuse him. A similar lack of serious consideration prompts her to send the valentine with its fatal words "Marry me" to Boldwood, and her vanity betrays her into marrying Troy at Bath, when he says he has seen someone prettier than her. Her impulsiveness and her teasing make her attractive, but her judgement is not sound.

    When she inherits the farm at Weatherbury, she determines to be independent, dismissing Bailiff Pennyways, and paying the men herself. She oversees farm affairs, such as the sheep-shearing and dipping. Her practical nature, her spirit and determination, come out on the night when she helps Gabriel cover the haystacks in the face of a thunderstorm.

The mistakes that Bathsheba makes eventually push her into a position of reliance on Gabriel Oak. Though his frankness hurts her, she has to turn to him when the sheep are "blasted", and when she is overcome with grief and shame at Troy's disappearance, so that Oak takes over the running of the farm, and is appointed bailiff. After Troy's death, she finally senses Oak's true value to her – that she needs a strong, honest man, and hints that he may propose to her. Finally, then, she surrenders her independence to him as someone stronger and more able to run her life.

Maggie Hobson would never do that. Her youth has been spent skirmishing with her father, and despite his insults she never gives an inch, even over the time of lunch:

HOBSON: Well, what about that dinner?
MAGGIE: It'll be ready in ten minutes.
HOBSON: You said one o'clock.
MAGGIE: Yes, Father. One for half-past. If you'll wash your hands it'll be ready as soon as you are.

Maggie is independent enough to propose to Willie, with her "Will Mossop, you're my man." She is firm and forthright, and she has the intelligence to seize all her opportunities, whether they are obvious, like Mrs. Hepworth's visit, or need imagination, like her father's fall down the Prosser's trap-door. She is a go-getter and she uses Willie as her path to success.

Sometimes, Maggie seems cold. When she proposes to Will, she says he is "a business idea in the shape of a man". She is capable of tricking her own father out of £500 (a fortune in those days) and setting firm conditions before she will look after him in his old age. She has, though, lived a hard life, and her feelings are present but below the surface. She will not marry Willie if he does not wish to, and when he says, "We'd not get much without there's love between us, lass," she replies, "I've got the love all right." Her feelings about her brass wedding ring show her to be a sincere person, and in the play she has been independent enough to teach Willie independence, too.

⑤ Nonetheless I prefer to her the equally independent but more passionate Jane Eyre.

Wider Reading Essay

Jane, too, has had a tough childhood, which enables her as a young woman to advertise and find herself a job in a distant part of the country. Her strength shows constantly – for instance, when she rescues Mr. Rochester from the fire, and when she flees to Derbyshire and starts a new life as a schoolmistress.

Jane's youth has also taught her the value of love, in the form of her closeness to Helen Burns. Helen has also taught her self-discipline, however, and this is what Jane needs when she falls for Mr. Rochester. The attraction is strong, and because of their class-difference it is often disguised as teasing. Her reactions to him are expressed physically, so that you can tell the strength of their physical attraction: when Rochester hints that their relationship must change, Jane writes "This was a blow, but I did not let it prostrate me." She is constantly on guard against her feelings, for she has strong principles and will not become his mistress.

She shows great strength in starting a new life after Rochester's attempted bigamy with her, and remarkable love and forgiveness when she returns to him after his wife's death and his disfigurement by a second fire.

⑥ In the novel, Jane's character is thoroughly tested: she is independent and disciplined, but still full of passionate and impetuous feelings. She has neither Bathsheba's tendency to give in to weakness, nor Maggie's tendency to shut out her warmer feelings. It is this balance of passion and good sense that makes me prefer Jane.

Notes
① *Introduction* mentions the texts in question and . . .
② *. . . the basic ideas* about them which are explored below.
③ *Development.* The fact that the next section is about *Far from the Madding Crowd* is signposted clearly.
④ Points are made as usual by quotations and references.
⑤ Contrasts between characters are stressed at the beginnings and ends of sections.
⑥ A *conclusion* paragraph draws the three sections together.
- Plan comparison essays in clear sections.
- Make comparisons and contrasts clear at the beginning and end of each section.
- Always write clear introductions and conclusions to comparison essays.

Creative Work in Wider Reading

It is harder here than in other sections to find creative ways for writing. Nonetheless, some essays can be written in the voice of a character in one book: what would he or she say, for instance, on meeting characters from other books? How would they react on reading these books or poems? Alternatively, you could write a piece in the form of a series of interviews with characters from books and poems, or with their authors. If you like this sort of writing, a little ingenuity will suggest a title to you.

The Value of Wider Reading

To do well at English Literature, you really have to enjoy what you are doing: only then will the imaginative responses on which the subject depends come freely to you. In giving you a section of assessment in which you have some control over what you read, Wider Reading and Open Study sections provide you with the opportunity to read things that you enjoy and can readily relate to. Try to shine in this part of your work.

Your teachers will hope, too, that this enjoyment will affect your life outside the Literature classroom. If you profit fully from the course, you should be much more able to enjoy reading and writing. In particular, you should be able to write more creatively for your GCSE English Language assessment and so boost your grade.

Index

Alliteration 72 – 3
Assessment 8, 42 – 5, 79 – 82
Assonance 72 – 3

Background (to plot) 26, 33 – 5
Background reading 9

Characterisation 18 – 19, 26, 28 – 33
Comedy 38
Comparisons 15 – 16
Connotation 14 – 15
Consonants 73
Coursework 8

Denotation 14
Description 19 – 20
Drama – see prose and drama

End-stopping 68
English Language courses 5
English Literature courses 5 – 8
Enjambement 68 – 9
Essays
  poetry 81 – 4
  prose and drama 43 – 5, 53 – 8
  wider reading 90 – 4
Examinations
  open-book 8

Genres 86

Heroes and heroines 87 – 8
Humour 38

Imagery 15 – 18
Irony 29, 38 – 9

Metaphors 15 – 16
Mood 18 – 19

Notes 39 – 40, 54
Novels 26 – 41, 42 – 63

Onomatopoeia 20, 73
Open-book examinations 8
Open Studies 7, 85 – 95

Passage questions 10 – 25, 43, 46 – 53
Pauses 67 – 9
Personifications 16
Plays 26 – 41, 42 – 63
Plot 27, 37 – 9

Poetry
  definition 64 – 5
  form and content 64 – 5
  techniques 65 – 74
  unseen appreciation 79 – 81
Prose and drama
  definition 7
  passage questions 25, 43, 47 – 53
  unseen appreciation 11 – 25

Quotations 25

Relationships 32 – 3
Religion 35
Rhyme 71 – 2
Rhythm 69 – 71

Sensuous language 19 – 20
Sentences
  length 20
Settings 33 – 5
Significance 50
Similes 15
Social background 34 – 5
Sound-play 20, 71 – 4
Stories 26 – 41, 42 – 63
Substitution test 15
Symbols 16 – 18
Synonyms 13 – 15

Themes 26, 35 – 7
Tone 18 – 19

Unseen Appreciation 11 – 25, 79 – 81

Verse 66 – 71
  end-stopping 68
  enjambement 68 – 9
  line-length 66 – 7
  pauses 67 – 9
  rhyme 71 – 2
  rhythm 69 – 71
Vowels 73

Wider reading 7, 85 – 95
  choosing texts and topics 86 – 90
  genres 86
  heroes and heroines 87 – 8
  themes 86 – 7
Words
  beliefs and feelings 14 – 15
  connotations 14 – 15
  denotations 14
  meanings 14 – 15
  sounds 20, 71 – 4
  substitution test 15